Thinking Bigger

The Essential Guide to Humanity's Greatest Future

Warren A. Musser

Hardback ISBN: 979-8-340718-02-0
Paperback ISBN: 979-8-218228-93-4
Ebook ISBN: 979-8-218228-96-5

Printed in the United States of America

Contents

Acknowledgements

I want to thank Muriel Castera Rawson, my mother, for without her financial support the present work would not have been possible. I also want to thank my wife, Elizabeth, and our two children, Diane and Kimberly, for their continuing love and for putting up with Dad's project that never seemed to end.

Many thanks also to physics professor Charles Shapiro of UC San Francisco and engineering professor Daniel DeBra of Stanford, both of whom offered helpful suggestions. Others who contributed significantly to this book include Hana May Dahl, Bradley Fisher, Pauline Fisher, Kimberly Musser, Donald Weeden, editors Margaret Manos and Brooks Becker, and, most particularly, two ex-Stanford University roommates Brock Fisher, a retired physician, and John Sargent, the retired head of Macmillan publishing.

Dedication

To humanity, the Milky Way's self-transforming, self- transcending species:

You are Calousian creators.

Commit fully to fulfilling your potential.

Go for it!

Anything less will severely diminish what you are.

Quote

The caterpillar eats and eats, unaware that in doing so it is transforming itself into a beautiful butterfly.

The human learns and learns.

WARREN A. MUSSER

Part 1

DOES OUR HUMAN PROGRESSIVE PROCESS HAVE A NATURAL SUMMIT, A GREATEST FUTURE?

1

WHY ARE WE HUMANS LOST? WHY DOES IT MATTER?

This book's purpose is not to explore humanity's near-term future. That has already been done by many authors. Instead, it's to identify our species' revolutionary greatest future. And, as you will see, to have any chance of reaching this greatest future, we must start for it now.

This Chapter is preparatory. Let's begin with two questions essential to this book's purpose. The first is: "What is our species' greatest achievement?" One possible candidate is our species' cooperative creation of languages, each with all its essential, made-up rules, the key to all human progress thereafter. Another possibility is our species' long success, so far, in continuing to survive.

But I think that the obvious answer to the question of our species' greatest achievement is really our Great Progression. By this I mean: the growth of knowledge, abilities, and tools that have transformed how we live, starting from our original condition as naked, sleeping-on-the-ground hunters and gatherers living off the plants and animals that nature produced, and proceeding up to the very different ways that the more advanced among us live today– socially, economically, and environmentally.

So why is our species' Great Progression so important? It's because, over the generations, it has made human lives, generally, ever bigger, richer, and better. In consequence, almost everything that we individual humans do today–how we communicate and travel, what we eat and how we get it, the work we do, where we sleep, and, really, how we live–is the product of our astonishing Great Progression.

Yes, we've advanced very far. And today, we live far longer, send rockets to Mars, transplant hearts and faces, use hand-held computers to phone friends and transact business.

The second question essential to this book's purpose is: "What is our species greatest failure?" The answer is that we still have no idea where this Great Progression of ours should ultimately take us in spite of the many generations participating in this Great Progression and the extraordinary advances in our knowledge, abilities, and the way we live.

Why Is Being Lost Such a Problem?

One big reason it's a problem is this: if we don't know where our progress should take us, we can't even be sure what we humans really are. After all, in the future, we may improve and keep improving our human bodies, so that they eventually become quite different from what we humans are today. If so, then we would be like caterpillars ignorant of their future butterfly form. And if our species' biggest and most important achievement is our Great Progression, and we still can't be sure of what we humans are, and we are presumably the ones in charge of this Great

Progression, then aren't these three realities kind of a problem?

And here's another problem from our being lost. We know the universe contains two trillion galaxies and unknown quadrillions of stars. But these structures are so enormous, so distant, and so different in character from our tiny lives on our relatively tiny planet that, unless we got hit by an asteroid, the existence of these galaxies and stars above (except our own star) seem completely irrelevant to our human lives.

But, as you will see, quite astonishingly, we relatively microscopic humans on our tiny blue dot don't just have a relationship with the universe. As you will see, it turns out that we humans play a most important role in how the universe actually progresses. In fact, our human role is just as essential to the progressing universe as that played by huge stars and colossal galaxies. So we remain lost not only about what we really are, but lost also about our true relationship with the universe.

So don't you think, as we fumble forward in our Great Progression, our species' greatest achievement, that our being lost about our universal role, in whatever part we play, could be a problem?

Because we remain lost, the character of our Great Progression becomes a problem, too. As briefly noted, it's the nature of this Progression that it keeps accelerating and growing ever more complex. This is because, as our knowledge keeps growing, it opens windows to more new knowledge, and the new knowledge keeps producing ever more new tools, new specialists, new products, and new services. So where previously all humans did the same hunt-and-gather jobs, and then almost everyone farmed, today, with the growth of knowledge, economies and societies have grown far larger and more complex, and people do tens of thousands of different kinds of jobs. In consequence, governance has become larger and more complex, too.

And, of course, the more we progress in the future, the more we can expect our Great Progression to continue both its accelerating and its increasing complexity. It's therefore evident that if our Great Progression is to continue and prosper, it will require large-scale management now and will require ever greater management in the future. Isn't this another problem made worse by our being lost?

But being lost about where our Great Progression should take us, about our species' greatest failure, is more than just a problem: it has allowed us to drift into an existential crisis. This crisis has a number of causes. I'll mention just three of them here. We'll consider the rest in this book's Part III.

Our Surging Human Population

The first cause of our existential crisis is our surging human population. It's characteristic of us humans to love sex, babies, and family. One problem is that because our individual human lives are so brief compared to our species' long existence, a great increase in our numbers hardly causes us any notice. These two facts make it difficult for us to rouse ourselves to the great danger of our human multiplication.

Here are some numbers:

In 3,000 BC, the start of the urban revolution, the world human population stood at about 20 million people. During the long previous hunt-and-gather times, the human population was far smaller.

In AD 1, the worldwide human population was 300 million. In 1800, 1,800 years later, 1 billion.

In 1927, 127 years later, 2 billion.

In 1974, 50 years later, 4 billion.

In 2022, 52 years later, 8 billion.

In 2054, 32 years later it will be, 10 billion.

To underscore how recent and extraordinary this massive increase in our human population is, your author was born in a world of only two billion people. Earth now holds six billion additional humans, and two additional billion more are expected by mid century.

What crises is our human population explosion causing?

Just think of all the additional houses these eight billion more than when I was born will need with all their additional contents. Think of all the food these eight billion additional people must have. Think of all the space they need, and how they and their activities are influencing all the other forms of life on our planet. And remember, our planet is of finite size. In consequence, there must also be some limit, some carrying capacity limit, to the number of humans who can live comfortably upon our planet without diminishing and/or destroying its natural wonders and its capacity to support us.

We recognize that not just humans, but all species have this tendency to multiply their numbers. Other aspects of the total environment, then, must have a strong tendency to keep the environment in balance by suppressing this growth. Consider the following examples: Simple algae, if they expand their numbers greatly in what is called an "algae bloom," suffer as a consequence with a severe population collapse. If we plant too many of the same crop in an area, they become susceptible to a blight that could kill most of them off. And if lion populations grow too far beyond their food source, many lions must starve. Even today, one billion humans, roughly one in eight, suffer from inadequate food and other necessities.

Furthermore, we are not just increasing our numbers, but we are also both living longer and raising living standards. And as our transportation and communication technologies advance, our world, in effect, shrinks ever smaller. This means that our impact on our environment is even greater than our numbers, altering it ever more to suit our wants and needs, as we use ever more energy and natural resources.

So far, our species, by such means as growing our food rather than just finding it, has found ways to keep increasing our numbers. But in doing so, as I will show, we have diminished our environment so rapidly and dangerously as to create a crisis.

Earth is finite and its biosphere delicate. At some point, and we've undoubtedly passed it, you cannot have both all humans enjoying higher living standards and an increasing number of humans. Yes, we can have more people for a time, but only if a few live in luxury and the rest suffer from ever lower living standards. But do we want this?

If we want all humans to share equally in the benefits of our growing knowledge and abilities, we must set a limit to the number of humans on Earth. And the more we progress, the smaller this number of living humans must be.

Has our population growth ceased? No, it's still growing, still a threat, still very much crisis-causing.

Climate Change Troubles

We've just noted the influence of our surging population on our environment. But another aspect of environmental deterioration is causing an existential crisis: it's climate change. Its warmer air causes more intense droughts. "Seventeen countries...home to a quarter of all humans, are using almost all the water they have. "Furthermore, "the warmer air also causes bigger and more violent storms and flooding rivers. It melts glaciers and raises oceans to flood coastal regions" (World Resources Institute: WRI). In consequence, A UN panel on biodiversity warns that..."global warming (is) a major driver of...an alarming one million plant and animal species...at risk of extinction worldwide..." (Intergovernmental Science-Policy Platform on Biodiversity and Ecosystem Services:IPBES).

"Climate change is already hurting the availability of food because of decreased yields and lost land from erosion, desertification, and rising seas, among other things." "Already more than 10 percent of the world's population remains undernourished"-that translates into some 770 million people.

"If global temperature rises 2 degrees above preindustrial levels, 100 million or more would suffer from hunger." Moreover, the longer policymakers wait to cut emissions, the harder it will be to prevent a global crisis. Waiting, delaying action...risks "irreversible loss in land eco- system functions and services required for food health, habitable settlements, and production" (Intergovernmental Science-Policy Platform on Biodiversity and Ecosystem Services: IPBES).

How are we doing? "The international community is falling far short of the Paris goals, with no credible pathway to 1.5 degrees C in place. The window is closing!...global temperatures can reach 2.8 degrees C by the end of the century (The UN environment programme: UNEP).

What kind of future do we want: an earthly biosphere that delights and supports us, or one that's increasingly damaged and threatening?

Has climate change stopped? No. It's still an increasing threat, still crisis-causing.

Our Tradition of Fighting Ever Bigger Wars With Ever More Destructive Weapons

For some 5,000 years, city states and the larger, more modern nations have been fighting each other incessantly with ever more destructive weapons. This tradition recently culminated in two World Wars. The last one killed 70 million people with machine guns, bombers, cannons, flame throwers, and atomic bombs. Now we seem to be preparing for World War Three–perhaps with China and its allies against the US and Europe–this time fighting with hydrogen bombs, each a thousand times stronger than the two that destroyed two cities and ended our Second World War. And, of course, we also have biological weapons, weapons guided by artificial intelligence, and intercontinental missiles.

Has this long tradition of fighting with ever more powerful weapons stopped?

Not yet. And it's obvious that it cannot continue because it already threatens our species' extinction.

Who Is in Charge?

The last problem I will mention that arises from our species being lost in our Great Progression is: who is in charge of our Progression? I noted above that we humans are "presumably" in charge of our greatest accomplishment. But is any person really in charge? Is any country in charge? Does our Progression have any international or planet-wide group of managers?

Of course not. No individual or group is presently in charge. Don't you think this may be a problem when our Great Progression is of our own creation, when it's accelerating and growing increasingly complex, and when, unlike our other big tasks, we've not yet attempted to manage this biggest and most important task of all? Our failure to manage, arising chiefly from our being lost, would seem to be the perfect way to prevent us from ever reaching that biggest, richest, best-possible future that our Great Progression makes available to us.

In sum, these are the reasons why being lost in our species' Great Progression is creating an existential crisis for our species. And these crisis conditions, far from helping us make the best of our Great Progression's future and continue our species' biggest and most important accomplishment, threaten instead to drive us ever sooner and more decisively to an early extinction.

So now let's start with a first main purpose of this book. It's to determine, if we can, whether our species' Great Progression, our species' greatest achievement so far, is an endless progression or has a natural summit, our greatest future.

How should we begin this difficult task? Let's start by clarifying what we humans really are. Why start in this area? The next chapter explains.

2

WHAT ARE WE HUMANS, REALLY? PART 1

A primary purpose in this book is to determine whether or not our species' long, Great Progression has a summit, our greatest future. The subject of our species' uniqueness is therefore important. If we don't understand what makes our species the summit species of Earth's biological evolution, we can have no solid basis for considering our species' purpose or future. After all, frogs, sparrows, and chimps, being different kinds of creatures from us, must have different futures. So, what is our species' primary character?

So far, we have not clearly identified the essence of our species' character. For example, we have typically identified ourselves in three ways. First, we are *Homo sapiens*, the "wise ones" among our taxonomic *Homo* group, and that's true. Second, we are tool users, and third, we are culture bearers and both of these latter categories are true, also.

However, the problem with these three primary characterizations of our species is that they are both incomplete and static.

They are incomplete in characterizing what we are, in explaining our primary progressive activity, because our growth also depends on additional characteristics, for example, that we are mobile, dexterous, curious, social, cooperative, and have oral and written language.

And these characterizations of us are static because they suggest that, like all other forms of Earth life, we change slowly through accidental mutations and natural selection.

If we had continued living as hunters and gatherers, this static characterization of us would suffice. But we haven't. As our knowledge has grown, we have profoundly changed how we live and, in this sense, altered what we are, too. So seeing ourselves over time makes it evident that we are not a static species; we are instead a most progressing species. Today, our knowledge is fast growing, and therefore it's fast changing how we live. We humans are dynamic creatures, not static ones.

Yes, we are bearers of culture, but when viewed longer term, we realize that we humans are also the creators of cultures, the changers of cultures, the expanders of cultures, and the destroyers of cultures. Similarly, we are not just tool users. More important to understanding what we are is that we are the creators of ever more wondrous kinds of extraordinary tools—from bridles for horses to self-driving cars to rocket ships.

As for being wise, we remain intelligent and discerning, but our "world," since hunt-and-gather days, has grown to planet-wide scale and become enormously complex. Compare, for example, a tribal village with one of today's megacities. In consequence, individuals today must spend the equivalent of a classical Roman's entire average lifetime (24 years) to graduate from college, just to get enough specialized and general knowledge to make their way successfully in the modern world.

How can we do all these things? It's because we have the mobility, senses, intelligence, and manipulative skill to create new knowledge.

Equally important, we also enjoy true language and later printing and the social cooperation that allows us to accumulate this knowledge socially and improve upon it. It's this new process of knowledge creation and knowledge accumulation socially rather than the older process of mutations and natural selection that distinguishes us from all other earthly organisms.

Our dynamic progression is not the consequence of the growth of wisdom. It's the result of the enormous growth of our knowledge, particularly our scientific and technological knowledge.

I therefore submit that what makes our species unique and the summit species of earthly biological evolution is that we are the first and only earthly species that can keep increasing its abilities over the generations. We do this through the new process of knowledge growth and adjustments rather than by the older biological process of mutations and natural selection. It's this characteristic that distinguishes us from all other earthly organisms.

Identifying this abilities-expanding characteristic of our species may surprise some. After all, neither you nor I invented the wheel. Obviously, only a tiny percentage of humans uncover new Science and Technology (SciTech). The rest of us contribute importantly by learning of the technology–e.g., the wheel–using it, and keeping the concept alive in our cultures for further possible use.

So in this longer time-frame focus, we can characterize ourselves as **abilities expanders.** What does this term mean? It suggests that as we keep increasing our abilities over time, we will transform how we live and, eventually, if we keep growing and changing, what we are.

This characterization of ourselves as abilities expanders may not sound so special, but it's what makes us unique among all living species. It's what makes humans the most dynamic species on Earth. It's what has us progressing. And progressing, as this book will make increasingly evident, is the paramount, long-term characteristic and task of our species.

The great problem with the traditional, static way of characterizing us humans–that we are wise, culture bearers, and tool users–is that it is most inappropriate and dangerous. It's most inappropriate, because it misses our species' most significant and unique quality, the quality that involves us in an accelerating, ever-more-complex progression, the quality that gives us the potential to become a self-transforming species.

This traditional, static characterization is dangerous because it tends to hide us from ourselves, and therefore to both inhibit and block us from perceiving our species' dynamic character. It therefore tends to keep us unchanging, to stop us from fulfilling our species' extraordinary potential. We won't strive for that natural expansion of ourselves. We won't become the higher beings our character urges us to become. We won't complete the self-transformation of our caterpillar state, so to speak, into our natural, future, beautiful, butterfly state. And we won't reach our species greatest future.

In sum, this static view of our species is not just inappropriate; it's going to prevent us humans from reaching our potential, natural, brilliant future.

Do we now really understand what we humans are?

No. This is just Part I of what we are. As you will see later, there is much more to us that we must learn about.

We want to understand where our species' Great Progression should take us. But is it possible to really understand our species' future without considerable knowledge of our species' past? Of course not. So in the next chapter, we'll briefly review our species' astonishing history.

3

HUMAN HISTORY: HOW DID OUR SPECIES PROGRESS?

We briefly mentioned aspects of human history in Chapter 1. Now we must examine it in more detail. Why must we understand this human history? Because this first step clarifies how our species progresses, and this knowledge in turn is essential to understand where our progress should take us.

In this chapter, we'll look at our human history, and then, in the next chapter, we'll examine the cause of our progression.

Human History

My interest in this book's subject began with my becoming aware of accelerating change in the human condition and, soon after, my increasing curiosity about where this process of change tended to take humanity. It's therefore appropriate here to ask: **Does accelerating change really exist?**

Yes, it does. And perhaps the best way to understand it is through a glance at human history. An understanding of human history, in turn, will help us better understand our species and its potential future. To emphasize accelerating change, I'll tell our human history as though it all took place in one year.

Note: Earth's history, starting 4.6 billion years ago, makes up roughly the last one third of universal history. Human history, if we consider it arising just 50,000 years ago, would make up 1 of 92,000 parts of Earth's history and 1 of 276,000 parts of universal history.

Fossils of humans with skeletons the same as ours first appeared in Africa between 195,000 and 160,000 years ago, and tools similar to the ones used then appear in north Africa some 300,000 years ago. But although some elements of modern behavior, e.g., the use of red ochre and stone blades, occurred early in this period, they're nothing compared to the advances that were seen in Europe beginning roughly 42,000 years ago, probably as the consequence of language improvement.

Let's review this 42,000 year history, pretending it all happened in one year.

From January 1 through June, July, August, and until the last days of September, we humans are naked*, homeless, hunters and gatherers. Small, self-sufficient groups of us, perhaps a dozen people–men, women, and children–wander around inside the tribe's territory seeking to gather the food that nature supplies. Typically, the men mostly hunt or scavenge larger animals, and the women and children collect small animal foods, such as insects and small mammals, and wild plant foods, such as fruits, vegetables, tubers, seeds, and nuts. At night, our ancestors sleep naked on the ground like foxes. They have to keep moving, because if they remain long in one place, they soon exhaust the easier-to-obtain foods in that location. For this reason, they own only what they can easily carry.

*Re. **Human hunters and gatherers (H&G) being naked.** Our species' H&G era was very long, starting some 300,000 years ago, and, of course, it continues in some places even today. H&G societies also lived in many part of the world under many different conditions. So when I speak of H&G humans being naked, I'm referring to how they dressed, in usual conditions, in their early days in the relatively warm African climate."*

The Agricultural Revolution

Then, some 11,000 years ago, the end of September in our one year history, the Agricultural Revolution begins. The new SciTech here is knowing how to raise plants and animals. Then, since humans no longer need to wander after food, we learn how to build cozy little huts in small settlements among our relatives. We increase our population, start wearing a little clothing, and enjoy village life. We now have chiefs and councilmen, but everyone in the villages at this time does the same agricultural work.

This Agricultural Revolution continues through October and into early November.

The Urban Revolution

In early November of our one year history of the world, but some 5,000 years ago in reality, the Urban Revolution begins in the especially fertile area of the Tigris and Euphrates river valley in Iraq, when advances in agriculture permitted populations to reach city size.

The cause is better farming methods in these fertile areas, particularly plowing with oxen and irrigation. The resulting larger food supply supports city states with some

50,000 inhabitants each, far too large now for kinship communities or for any individuals to know everyone.

This large society requires management. The tribal chief becomes a great king and lives in an impressive palace, with household attendants and, for defense against neighboring cities, officers and professional soldiers.

This costs money, so citizens must be taxed, and bureaucrats must collect taxes and account for what they collect and where the collected property goes. Similarly, those who import and export products far from the city must make verifiable agreements with distant sources and markets. So scribes appear, keeping written financial records that, eventually, become more detailed and expressive.

With urban life, the economy grows more complex. In addition to farmers, kings, scribes, and soldiers, we have pastoralists to care for the animals we raise for food and transportation; caravan, boat and raft people, who transport our products; importers and exporters; merchants in the marketplace; brick makers for building houses up to three stories high and public buildings; copper and bronze metal workers; and pottery manufacturers–all these items made in the home or small workshops.

New sources of energy at this time include wind (for sailing); animals (for riding and pulling, carrying and plowing); and falling water (to power grain and timber mills).

The list of new SciTech underlying the Urban Revolution includes shipbuilding (boats, rafts); coinage for trade; simple metallurgy; writing; house building; public buildings and architecture; more complex weapons (such as swords, spears, and shields); and more elaborate clothing.

Society becomes stratified and more complex. The former tribal chief is transformed into a managing priest and then into a great king, with his bureaucrats–advisers, managers, scribes, accountants, tax collectors, and soldiers. And, of course, there are the food producers: farmers and the animal-raisers.

Beliefs become more sophisticated. Heretofore, humans have believed that their world–both its animate and inanimate aspects–is governed by spirits. Magic and tradition are employed to help humans get along with all the supernatural beings around them.

Now, with the rise of urban life, humans dominate plants, animals, and even rivers as their irrigation systems put water where it's wanted. With society stratified, kings in their palaces dominate over common farmers. Therefore, for the first time, it begins to make sense to think of the world as governed by a hierarchical society of gods in human form, rather than just by spirit-beings.

At around December 23 in our one year history, ancient Greeks experience the Age of **Pericles**. On December 27, Columbus "discovers" America.

The Industrial Revolution: Preparation

Around December 29 in our one year history, the Industrial Revolution begins. This revolution dates roughly from 1750 to 1900. This great change in humans' lives could only occur after the previous few hundred years, during which members of our species gained the **self-assurance** to question previously held truths and find new ones for themselves.

Examples of this new world that led up to the Industrial Revolution include the following:

In 1419, **Prince Henry of Portugal** starts a school of navigation, map-making, and science to train his students in the daring task of sailing from Portugal down and around the west coast of Africa. These sailors think they risk horrible death from monstrous sea creatures or from falling off the edge of the Earth. Through a long sequence of steps, each ship sails down as far as previous ships, then, after going only a little further, the sailors grow so fearful that they turn around and return home. But gradually ships, maps and navigation improve.

In 1492**, Columbus** accidentally discovers the New World of the Americas while bravely trying to access the riches of the Old World-India-by sailing, not east, but west.

In 1543, **Copernicus** publishes his new theory that the sun, not the Earth, is the center of the universe.

That same year, surgeon **Andreas Vesalius** publishes his book of detailed anatomical drawing of the human body, derived from his personal human dissections. He holds the strange belief that surgery should be based not on ancient ideas but on anatomy, and that anatomy should be understood through careful observation of the human body.

Finally, around this time, a new scientific method takes hold, one based on experiment, reason, and a more mechanistic world view. For example, in 1660 the world's first scientific society, the Royal Society of London, is founded following a lecture by astronomer **Christopher Wren**. The Society's purpose is to promote the new

"Physico-Mathematical Experimental Learning." And in 1687, **Sir Isaac Newton's** *Principia* is published, a revolutionary new mathematical description of how the solar system works. Newton's other accomplishments include inventing calculus and the reflecting telescope; proposing the idea that gravity is a universal force; and identifying the three laws governing motion that provided the basis of classical mechanics.

These new, more accurate ways of looking at Earth and the solar system, and the new scientific method, encourage thinkers and inventors to make new discoveries themselves, activities that lead to the Industrial Revolution.

The Industrial Revolution

We'll focus here on the first part of the Industrial Revolution (IR), 1750 to 1850, which starts in Britain and spreads to Continental Europe and North America.

The IR's new source of energy is the burning of coal and coke. Coke is to coal what charcoal is to wood. In both instances, the natural material is partly burned, which drives off impurities and makes the original material less smelly, more porous, and hotter burning.

The IR's new material is inexpensive iron. England has lots of iron, but it contains too many impurities, so in the early days, English iron is imported from Sweden.

Iron ore, depending on where it is mined, is a mixture of iron, oxygen, water, and other minerals. To remove the ore's impurities, the ore must be smelted, that is, the iron in the ore heated to the melting point. At first, smelting is done on open hearths; later, blast furnaces are used. The blast furnace turns out ingots of pig iron with 6%

impurities, including 2 to 5% carbon. But this pig iron is too brittle for most uses.

The next advance is to turn pig iron efficiently into wrought iron, a more malleable, easier to work material. In 1784, **Henry Cort** and his son do this by improving "puddling." The hot liquid iron is poured into a small pool, then stirred with iron rods as warm, oxygenated air passes over it. This process burns the impurities down to 1% and carbon to .02%. Wrought iron's great advantage is that it can be shaped into bars or rolled into sheets.

This new, inexpensive, and abundant wrought iron appears everywhere in England: iron fences and iron grates on the windows protect houses in cities, iron posts on the sides of streets temporarily hold horses, iron wheels carry the horse-drawn vehicles. These wheels on the stone streets make such a racket that when shop doors open, everyone just automatically stops talking, and only resume when the doors shut. And, of course, iron produces the railroad steam engines that ride on iron tracks that cross iron bridges and go through iron tunnels. In the 1850s, the Bessemer process makes the large-scale production of steel possible.

The new coal and iron help create the IR's new power source when, in 1769, **James Watt** creates a practical, efficient steam engine. Heretofore, except for the wind and falling water, human power had been restricted to the muscles of humans and animals. In consequence, goods were made by hand, in small quantities, in the home or in small shops. Now they are mass-produced by machinery, in large quantities, in big plants powered by massive, noisy, and smokey steam engines. The spinning of the engine's axle, transferred by complex systems of rods and belts, can spin or otherwise operate virtually all of a factory's many small manufacturing devices.

And, of course, steam engines also power railroads and, later, steam ships. So the steam engine not only creates large factories, but also new, large-scale methods of production and large distribution–all advancing a world wide economy. One of the many benefits of this new power source is a new material: machine produced cloth.

Before the IR, cloth, such as wool, was cleaned, spun into thread, then woven into fabric in the home, an important source of extra income for the farming family. In 1733, **John Kay's** "flying shuttle" allows one person to weave cloth on a loom rather than two. In 1764, **James Hargreaves'** "spinning jenny" can spin thread on eight spindles at once. These inventions help English farming families increase wool cloth production in their homes.

But then three inventors begin using water power to advance cloth making. In 1769, **Richard Arkwright** invents the "Water Frame" spinning machine that produces tougher thread than the Jenny. In 1779, **Samuel Crompton's** "Mule" produces wool thread that is both fine and tough. And in 1785 Rev. **Edmund Cartwright's** "Power Loom" turns this better thread into woolen cloth. By 1833, 85,000 power looms operate in England.

As for cotton cloth, England buys it mostly from India, but in 1789, **Eli Whitney** in the United States invents the cotton gin, which mechanically removes the cotton seeds. England imports this abundant cotton from America. Then, in big factories in big cities, England's steam engines power both the spinning and weaving to produce abundant and inexpensive cotton cloth, and later, woolen cloth. As a consequence, many farming families lose this source of income, which tends to force women and children, too, into those huge factories.

Agriculture during the IR becomes more productive. Though people know virtually nothing of genes, **Robert Bakewell** and others, in the 1750s, help start the transformation of sheep and cattle by managing animals breeding. Specifically, they mate the best animals–from their point of view–with the best. As a consequence sheep weight jumps from 28 to 80 pounds, cattle from 370 to 800 pounds.

In addition, farmers increase production by planting crops in rows and frequently overturning the soil between the rows. Land, then, is periodically allowed to remain fallow-unused-in order to regain productivity. **"Turnip" Townsend** urges the planting of turnips on the fallow land, which provides winter food for animals. Finally local farmers lose the commons, lands they had long used for feeding their animals. Workers are reduced to tenant farmers on lands now owned by others.

The result is more food produced by fewer people, and the rest of the people forced into factories.

Regarding transportation during the IR, around 1800, **John McAdam** and others begin to create better roads called turnpikes. They cover the formerly muddy, rutted, dirt roads with a hard surface of crushed rock.

The new iron and the steam engines revolutionize long-distance transportation over land, first in England, and then all over the world. The new steam engine powers the new trains of railways that make travel faster, cheaper, and far more comfortable. Of course, horses remain essential for getting to and from the stations or any other local destinations.

Late in this English IR, steam engines also begin to revolutionize water travel. Instead of the uncertainties of the wind power on sails, ships now start employing the more reliable steam-engine power. In 1807, in the United States, **Robert Fulton's** *Clermont,* using a Watt manufactured steam engine, starts paddle-wheeling passengers on the Hudson River between New York City and Albany. In London in 1858, **Isambard Kingdom Brunel** launches another steam ship, the *Great Eastern,* the biggest ship so far produced. With a double iron hull and 692 feet long, it carries 4,000 passengers. Its steam engine powers both a paddlewheel and a screw propeller, and, for good luck, the vessel also sports sails.

During the IR, England's navy, with its two-or three-decked ships and many cannons per deck, for broadside firepower, rules the waves.

At the start of the IR, communication is by voice, mail, and print, and travels at the speed of horses. But then, thanks to Watt, it begins traveling at the speed of steam engine powered trains. In 1844, **Samuel Morse**, the inventor of the Morse code, creates the first commercial long distance telegraph, its wire running from Washington to Baltimore. In 1866, the first transatlantic cable is established. In consequence, during the Civil War, **Abraham Lincoln** becomes the first American president able to keep in daily contact with his dispersed generals. Finally, steam powered printing presses make cheap newspapers and books possible, and push the novel to become a major art form.

This far faster and longer-distance communication system revolutionizes long-distance communication and knits the world closer together.

The IR's new technologies create a new economy: capitalism. Before the IR, production was small-scale and in the home. Now factories are big, because they are powered by the big new steam engines and all the mechanical devices connected to them. They need large buildings and large supplies of coal, and are operated by many people who must be paid.

Who can afford to buy and operate these factories? Not many-unless individuals pool their money. So we have the rise of the new capitalists raising money for new joint stock corporations.

These new large companies have managerial hierarchies, division of labor, sales organizations, and workers, so the IR creates more specialization.

As for the IR's social impact, the revolutions in communication and transportation bring more territory and more people under organization. By its end, the advanced industrial nations, with their great new wealth and resulting military power, acquire many less-advanced countries to create empires: British, Dutch, German, and American. These changes take us closer to a global society.

Before the IR, the center of English life was the village, a row of thatched cottages along a single street. The increased wealth created by the new industries now leads to a population increase. At the start of the IR, in 1750, England's population was 6.5 million; by 1901 it rose to 32.5 million. And with factories and commerce now located in cities, the population, too, moves into the cities. In 1750, three-quarters of the English population is rural; by 1901, over three-quarters is urban. These new industrial cities are larger and more crowded; with coal fires everywhere, they are also dark and sooty.

The IR changes the class system, too. In 1750, the aristocratic, land-owning wealthy class ruled England's government; a tiny middle class was made up of doctors, lawyers, and other professionals; and the rest of the population made up the large agricultural working class. By 1900, the land-owning class continues, but now the IR has created a new class: those enterprising, often self-made men who created, owned, and operated the factories, foundries, and mines. Many became as wealthy as the landed aristocrats, and this gave them political power, as well.

The working class–now without land, property, or secure employment–is made much larger by the addition of women and children. Clocks become essential, for employees must all start and stop work at the same time, in harmony with the steam engine's schedule. Since the workers lack unions, they work long hours, often under terrible working conditions. The family weakens.

The IR influences housing. The new city dwellers, just as they had when living in the countryside, inhabit houses without running water or indoor bathrooms. To get water, residents must walk with a bucket down the street to the nearest public hand pump, then carry the heavy load back, perhaps up several stories to their apartment. As for bathroom needs, people use the back lot with everybody else, and, at night, a bed pot. The latter is then emptied out the window into the street below, with its passing wagons and pedestrians, the contents joining the abundant horse manure there. At night, lighting continues to be by candles and whale oil lamps.

Perhaps the highlight of the IR in Britain is **Prince Albert's** Crystal Palace Exposition of 1851. It takes place in a giant glass-enclosed building in Hyde Park, and displays "The Works of Industry of All Nations." Some six million people attend.

Result: Ideas

The American Revolution in the first half of the 1760s started the movement to replace kings with democracy or, as Abraham Lincoln said, "government of, by, and for the people." In 1776, **Adam Smith**, in his work *The Wealth of Nations,* makes the new point that the major source of national wealth is no longer agriculture, but trade and commerce. In 1789, the French Revolution begins with the slogan "Liberty, Equality, Fraternity" and later extends to the killing of the king and queen. But the revolution degenerates and **Napoleon Bonaparte** takes power and wages wars around Europe. In 1790, **Edmund Burke**, shocked by all the death and damage from the French effort, writes in his *Reflections on the French Revolution* that the English system, with its king and parliament, has considerable merit after all.

The same IR communication and transportation advances that help create imperialism also help create nationalism. Finally, in 1848, the problems endured by factory workers prompt **Karl Marx** and **Friedrich Engels** to write about the class struggle in *The Communist Manifesto.* In 1850, **Charles Darwin's** *On the Origin of Species* introduces the concept of biological evolution.

In sum, the IR supplanted human-made, hand-made work with machine work. This shift changed the entire nature of society and economic life.

Note, I've named many inventors above, as though all these IR advances were the sole creation of a few single individuals. Yes, these individuals were important, but the advances were more truly the result of a new attitude, a new self-assurance, that gave many individuals, in many locations, the courage to find new ways to make things better. This new attitude is characteristic of the Industrial Revolution.

The Modern Age

The Modern Age begins on December 31, the last day of our one-year human history, just before noon–the year 1900 by the common calendar. Since the reader already knows a great deal about the modern period, we needn't cover much of it here.

This period includes two World Wars and the establishment of the first world-wide organizations to help prevent wars: the League of Nations and, later, the United Nations. But its most significant feature is its soaring growth of SciTech and other knowledge.

In energy, electricity becomes the dominant energy, and it is powered through most of this period by falling water, coal, petroleum, and later, partly by nuclear fission. But recently, due to climate change, coal and petroleum are beginning to be phased out, replaced by growing solar, wind, and, hopefully soon, nuclear fusion.

In power devices, motors (powered by electricity) and engines (powered by fossil fuels and chemicals) are both of great importance, but the use of the latter, except in rocket engines, will sharply decline as people become more aware of climate change.

In transportation, in the mid 1880s, competitors **Karl Benz** and then **Gottlieb Daimler** build the first practical gasoline-powered automobiles. Horses and other large animals begin to lose their long utility and so their numbers. In 1903, the **Wright brothers** succeed with their first powered flight. During the last four hours of our one-year history, all else quickly follows: widespread electric power; radios; plastics; microchips; electric and gas stoves and microwave ovens; refrigerators; television sets and programming; dishwashers; supermarkets; antibiotics; genetics and gene repairs; transplants; trips to the moon and other solar system bodies; computers and the Internet and smartphones. New telescopes, now observing in all parts of the electromagnetic spectrum, provide revolutionary new knowledge of the universe; microscopes reveal revolutionary molecular details of how cells work; and giant particle colliders identify subatomic components.

In short, **our history makes accelerating change strikingly evident.** It's as though we have been traveling in a car that has steadily increased its speed, and now clocks 80 miles an hour.

The big advantage to accelerating progress is that it advances us rapidly towards our long Great Progression's brilliant Summit, if it exists. The big disadvantage with increasing speed, as automobile drivers know, is that it accelerates the number of decisions faced per unit of time and so tends to punish bad decisions with escalating severity.

Now that we've briefly reviewed human history, our next question to find our species' astonishing purpose must be: **How does our species' long Great Progression actually**

work? As noted, this knowledge is obviously essential if we are going to understand where our progression should take us.

4

HOW DOES OUR SPECIES' LONG, GREAT PROGRESSION WORK?

Why should we know how our species' abilities-expanding progression–its long Great Progression–works? Because if we don't know how the progression works, we have no basis for identifying its best-possible future or our species' astonishing purpose.

I'll begin with an example. As noted, our species began as hunter-gatherers, who, organized into small bands, had to keep wandering, because they soon consumed all the easy-to-get food in any one area. This wandering strongly influenced what these early humans could own. They could really own only what they could conveniently carry. Having neither houses nor clothing, at night they slept naked on the ground like foxes do.

Then they became farmers and learned to raise plants and animals. This allowed them to give up wandering, sleep in protective huts in small villages near their fields, and start wearing clothing and owning more possessions.

How does our abilities-expanding progression work? I'll first give a brief answer and then provide helpful detail.

Abilities expansion is complicated, but essentially it works like this:

First, we increase our knowledge–especially SciTech knowledge, a term here that encompasses all STEMM knowledge; in other words, it includes in addition to science and technology, engineering, mathematics, and medicine. As a consequence, this knowledge usually expands our abilities. Think, for example, of **Thomas Edison** creating the electric light bulb.

Second, we live with the new knowledge or product and adjust to it. For example, to bring light, for the first time, to the people in a small district of Manhattan, Edison must get the people and government there to allow the necessary poles and lines to be constructed to bring the new electric power into each house. This task also requires a big electrical generator and financing. People love the new lighting. As this technology spreads, the market for candles and the killing of whales for their lamp oil starts to fall drastically.

But even more important, this second part of our abilities-expanding progression is where SciTech and other knowledge spreads from those who create the new knowledge, abilities, techniques, and the like, out into the society, cultures, the world where this new knowledge is maintained and accumulated. It's what keeps our species progressing instead of just changing.

Third and finally, these new conditions create the basis for the growth of still more new knowledge and abilities. For example, once houses have electric power, inventors can create many additional uses for this power. Examples include electric door bells, electric toasters for slices of bread, and radios. **Nikola Tesla** and **George Westinghouse** then devise a better way of transmitting electrical power, and their alternating current replaces Edison's direct current.

This circular progression of (A) creating new SciTech and abilities, (B) maintaining, accumulating and adjusting to these new accomplishments socially and then (A') creating more new SciTech and abilities, is basically how our abilities-expanding progression advances.

But why is SciTech the chief progressive factor? After all, in our individual lives, many other kinds of knowledge exist: for example, those relating to our families, our work, and our entertainments.

But for the long-term progression of our species, SciTech is the most progressive factor because it keeps directly expanding our abilities. It's what allows us to raise plants, to invent wheels, steam engines, and cellphones, and to improve our health.

The proof that SciTech is our abilities-expanding progression's primary knowledge is in what would happen if we took all SciTech away. For starters, we would lose our modern transportation abilities: bicycles, cars, trains, airplanes, etc. Now, if we wanted to go somewhere, we would have only our legs to take us there. Next, take away our communication abilities, like megaphones, telephones, newspapers, magazines, books, radios, TVs, and cellphones.

Now if we wanted to speak with someone or get information, like whether a local fire is still spreading, we must again use our legs to walk (or run) to find someone with reliable current knowledge of the fire or inspect the fire for ourselves.

Then, let's take away our SciTech-based household appliances—our dishwashers, refrigerators, stoves, hot water heaters, space heaters, air conditioners, etc. Then take away the house itself–its foundation, flooring, walls, siding, windows, doors, and roof. Now we are homeless. And, because the wheel has not been invented, nor the cotton gin, nor the sewing machine, we have no real clothing. At night, therefore, we must sleep naked on the ground. Finally, take away all the SciTech that fills our supermarkets with food. Now if we want to eat or drink we must walk about, trying to find the foods and liquids that nature supplies.

You can see that if we took away all SciTech, and all evidence of SciTech, we would be forced back to living the hunting-and-gathering life of our ancient ancestors. This is why SciTech is our species' chief progressive factor. It underscores the fact that the great bulk of things we have and do today are directly or indirectly the result of SciTech growth. After all, to write poetry you need paper and a pen, pencil, or computer. And to compose music, you need the writing materials, the musical instruments with all their different sounds, and perhaps the auditorium.

There are many complexities in the laws of our abilities-expanding progression that result in SciTech growth and that guide particular SciTech growth, and many more to account for the consequences of SciTech growth, but what's evident is that without this SciTech growth our abilities-expanding progression could not advance.

Now let's look into **a primary question of this book**: whether or not our ability-expanding progression, i.e., our long Great Progression, the biggest and most important achievement of our species, has a natural Summit.

Does Our Species' Long Great Progression Have a Greatest-Future Summit?

Since the chief progressive factor in our human progress is SciTech growth, whether our Great Progression has a summit or not depends upon whether there are limits to the benefits of SciTech growth or not.

This is one of the most important points in this book, because it's what makes finding the natural, universal Summit of our abilities-expanding evolution possible.

It's difficult today to accept limits to SciTech growth because this growing knowledge keeps providing us with so many surprising new abilities. Accepting limits also seems difficult because an advance in one area can often produce quite unexpected advances in very different areas. Who, for example, would suspect that the arcane SciTech of shaping bits of hot glass would turn out to reveal, in the form of microscopes and telescopes, not only the existence of invisibly tiny forms of life on Earth, but also new planets and moons in the solar system and, of course, trillions of galaxies? Finally, scientists and others tend to strongly agree with **Vannevar Bush**, the wise science adviser to presidents Roosevelt and Truman, who declared just science to be "an endless frontier."

If the future of our advancing, self-developing progression depends upon our knowing all SciTech, then, since SciTech growth is infinite, there can be no particular future ahead–just incessant, increasing growth, providing that we keep growing SciTech.

Then where will SciTech take us? Do we face an infinite progression, or does our Great Progression have a natural end point, a Summit?

Here is the **crucial point.** Even if SciTech can grow forever, this does not mean that this growth can keep enlarging a particular ability forever. For example, we can imagine that growing SciTech in the future will keep reducing the travel time between San Francisco and Paris, but it seems unreasonable to expect that this growth can continue to reduce the travel time over this distance forever. Limits like this one, which prevent ever-growing SciTech from ever-increasing specific abilities such as travel speed, are the key to the existence of our progression's Summit and so also to our discovering it.

Therefore, if we look not at all possible SciTech growth, but focus instead on particular benefits of SciTech growth that are important to us humans for completing our self-development–like those that significantly expand our abilities, such as increasing travel speed–then a particular greatest future begins to emerge. This occurs where SciTech growth of certain important abilities eventually becomes as great as universal conditions allow. Once an ability growth reaches this condition, becomes maximized, its growth thereafter, of course, becomes impossible. For example, once you can truly maximize travel speed from San Francisco to Paris, you can never go faster, no matter how much SciTech thereafter grows or how much intelligence may increase.

Therefore, to find whether our abilities-expanding progression can have a Summit, a greatest future, we must focus not just on SciTech growth itself, but also on the SciTech growth most important to our human species fulfilling its extraordinary potential by maximizing us humans.

To find out whether or not our species' long Great Progression has a brilliant Summit, we must be clear about what kind of progression, or evolution, we chiefly participate in. Is it our great abilities-expanding progression or is it still our biological evolution? To find out, let's see how these two evolutions differ.

5

HOW DO OUR ABILITIES-EXPANDING PROGRESSION AND OUR BIOLOGICAL EVOLUTION DIFFER?

Let's now note that there are two views of the relationship between biological evolution and our species' great abilities-expanding progression. One view is that our species' great abilities-expanding progression, with its changes in how we live, is just our species' way of adapting to the biological evolution that governs all of Earth's other living species. We humans are biological beings, after all. The other view is that our species' Great Progression is its own distinctively separate process in the progressing universe.

Why do we need to choose one of these viewpoints? It's because we are trying to understand where our progressing human evolution should take our species. Therefore, we need to be very clear about the kind of evolution that we find ourselves chiefly participating in, because these two evolutions differ considerably. When attempting to see ourselves in a universal context, I think it makes more sense to view our human evolution as separate from biological evolution and as a more advanced stage in the universe's long progression of stages.

Why? Six reasons:

First, because these two evolutions advance in different ways.

Our human evolution advances through (A) SciTech knowledge growth, (B) its social maintenance and accumulation and adjustments to this growth and then (A') more SciTech growth. Biological evolution advances though accidental mutations and selection, for example, where any favorable mutations give those individuals a reproductive advantage.

Second, the two evolutions produce different kinds of entities. Biological evolution produces cells, organs, species, ecosystems, etc. Human evolution produces cities, roads, cars, railroads, airplanes, rocket ships, bridges, alloys, plastics, computers, medicines, etc., as well as increasingly empowered humans–very different kinds of products.

Third, biological evolution produces different kinds of species, including more advanced species; human evolution produces the increased abilities of one species.

Fourth, biological evolution has no management and no way to produce it to advance itself (the human part, of course, excepted). It advances simply through the interaction of natural factors, like stellar evolution and the other previous evolutionary stages. Human evolution, in contrast, not only can produce management to advance, but eventually can't succeed without it.

For example, in human evolution, even if one person has the inventive idea, e.g., Edison and the light bulb, it will take a small managed group to perfect it, and then a much larger managed group to make the idea a reality. This larger managed group has to raise the necessary money, get the public's support for the project, build the power generators (in the case of the light bulb), and string the wires along streets from the generators into each house. Also required, of course, are organized communities, managed by mayors and governors, etc., to see that the wires are placed appropriately and not stolen or cut down. This is why progress in human evolution requires management.

Fifth, the two evolutions, long term, yield quite different summit products. Biological evolution produces us humans, the first biological species on Earth that can keep increasing its abilities over the generations through knowledge growth. Human evolution, as you will see, transforms us humans into more advanced universal beings and their advanced systems. (We'll discuss this more in Chapter 13.)

Sixth, as human evolution advances, we humans become ever more able to deliberately alter the genes of animals, plants, and ourselves, as compared with biological evolution's accidentally-produced mutations. Therefore, in human evolution, our species is increasingly implementing biological evolution's mutations and selections on other species and, increasingly, on ourselves. In consequence, as human evolution produces new kinds of roses, dogs, chickens, etc., biological evolution loses its long-term earthly role as the sole producer of new kinds of life.

These are the reasons I think human evolution should be considered an equal and separate kind of universal evolution from biological evolution. Note also that chemical evolution, which led to first life, similarly advances differently and produces different products from either biological evolution or human evolution.

You now know how different biological evolution and our species' great abilities-expanding evolutions are, and why the abilities-expanding evolution, is the chief one that our unique new species participates in.

But now, another question. We are trying to determine if our Great Progression has a natural Summit, humanity's greatest future. The Summit, in turn, will be determined by limits or maximums to the benefits of SciTech growth. So the question is: what areas should we attempt to maximize to prove that our progression has this Summit? That's the subject of the next chapter.

6

WHAT SUBJECTS SHOULD WE ATTEMPT TO MAXIMIZE? WHY WERE THEY CHOSEN?

To review, we humans differ from all other earthly species because we are able to deliberately expand our abilities–the kinds of things we can do –over the generations through knowledge growth. It's this characteristic that has our species participating in our long Great Progression.

Our twin goals here are first, to grow our SciTech to make the most of what we humans are, and, therefore, second, to select a cluster of subjects that are both important enough and can be maximized to establish a Summit.

I eventually decided that we should grow as far as possible two parts of ourselves: our Seven Fundamental Abilities and our bodies and minds. I'll introduce the final third part of us humans, the how-we-live part, later.

Note that these categories–fundamental abilities and bodies and minds–are crucial not just to our species' future, but would be crucial to the future of any other beings like us, if they exist, throughout the universe. I'll first identify these categories and then explain why I chose them.

Seven Fundamental Abilities

Since we can never know everything and since it's our own development that chiefly concerns us here, let's identify and focus on abilities that–long term–are fundamental to us humans.

The challenge here is to choose abilities that are, because of their great breadth and depth, both important to us as self-developing beings and essential for reaching and enjoying our progression's Summit, our greatest future. In other words, they must be abilities that growing SciTech can both increase and maximize. Why are these two conditions important? Because it's the great growth and the limits to that growth that will identify the Summit of each ability and of all the seven chosen abilities together.

Choosing just one ability, such as transportation, as a test for the existence of a Summit of our abilities-expanding evolution would be inadequate. Choosing two is little better. Yet we don't want to choose a large, ungainly number.

So what fundamental abilities should we consider?

Since maximizing our fundamental abilities will be difficult, I have limited their number to seven. They are: (1) the elemental realm; (2) the biological realm; (3) the astronomical realm; (4) communication; (5) transportation; (6) access to energy; and (7) power devices.

Why did I choose these particular seven abilities?

As noted, I've chosen these seven abilities for their importance and for the great breadth and depth of their influence on our species both now and in the future. The first three concern our primary environments: our elemental, biological, and astronomical environments. These areas are obviously important to us now and we can expect them to be important as well to the advanced beings of the future.

The (1) elemental realm covers all the universe's inanimate local entities. To simplify for present purposes, however, we will consider only small earthly items. This makes sense because, if we can master these smaller entities, then, since larger entities are usually made of them, we are well on the way to knowing how to make the larger entities.

Regarding the (2) biological and (3) astronomical realms, these categories are obviously enormous. The biological realm encompasses all life on Earth and perhaps on nearby astronomical sites as well. The astronomical realm has importance now–e.g., in the danger of asteroids, and in considering the moon and Mars as future habitats–and we will experience even more such habitats in the future.

(4) Communication and (5) transportation. What is the great importance of these two fundamental abilities? It is that when growing SciTech meets the limits of its benefits in these two realms, it will also have reached the maximum size of the sphere within the universe that intelligent beings can directly influence over a reasonable length of time.

Regarding (6) energy, the amount of cheap energy available is important. It tends to determine use per year and therefore life-style. People may not use all they have, but they cannot access more than they have. Presumably, those at the abilities-expansion Summit will enjoy an abundance of energy. It will provide the power for all the things they do. The greater the energy abundance, the easier it is to produce more goods and services and engage in giant tasks. Energy runs our engines and motors, our electric and electronic appliances, and our factories and mines.

Finally, I chose (7) power devices (e.g. engines and motors). These devices transform energy into motion or kinetic energy, and therefore they drive all the devices of our modern world and will undoubtedly drive even more kinds of devices in the future.

When our distant ancestors wanted to exert a force, they had to rely solely on their own muscles and later on those of dogs, horses, and oxen. Today, our inanimate power devices crank out energy, dig our gardens, refrigerate our food, heat and ventilate our homes, help to make our products, move dirt for roads or dams, and transport us to the moon. In the future, power devices will range in size from the submicroscopic or nano-scale all the way up to the astro-scale.

Are these Seven Fundamental Abilities sufficient categories to identify our abilities-expanding evolutionary Summit, our greatest future? By way of answer, suppose that a knowledgeable friend of yours thinks not, and wants to add, say, two more fundamental maximizable abilities. I submit that all the knowledge, tools, and techniques that must be acquired to maximize the chosen seven abilities and ourselves are so powerful, and cover such a broad and deep understanding and control over the entities of the local universe, that the people mastering them could, in a short time, also maximize any additional maximizable abilities that this knowledgeable friend might choose. That's why I think maximizing the Seven Fundamental Abilities and our bodies and minds (and, later, how we live) suffices.

Now let's look at the possible maximizing of our bodies and minds.

The Influence of Continuing SciTech Growth on Human Minds and Bodies

The improvement and possible maximization of our human bodies and minds is obviously primary in fulfilling our species' potential. But should we do it? Many will consider this task unethical and dangerous. At one extreme, it could create strange, sick individuals, and, at the other, a class of superior, perhaps ruling beings. But remember, we humans are ability-expanders. Ability-expanding is our species' unique characteristic, the one that has us progressing. And up to now, we've certainly done whatever our advancing knowledge lets us do to repair ourselves. For example, we have developed painkillers, learned how to conduct surgeries on broken parts, and to employ transplants, both artificial and natural (the latter from other humans and animals).

The main reason we have not yet made considerable improvements to our bodies and minds is that we have always lacked the necessary knowledge to do so. But now that knowledge is rapidly becoming available. For example, we can now find out if we have particular defective genes, and we will soon be able to replace these defective genes with good ones–if not in ourselves soon, unquestionably in our descendants' conceptions. And in the future, our growing technology will be certain to open up the possibility of giving us improved genes and new kinds of genes.

This category covers knowledge of how to fulfill the potential of the human body and mind. I chose this category since the inevitable growth of this ability in the future is too important and too interesting to omit. Furthermore, it's fundamental to understanding what we humans will be, and so, in this larger view, it is fundamental to what we humans really are. This category helps clarify, so to speak, not just our caterpillar present, but our butterfly future as well.

Obviously, the more changes we make here, the more we will transform ourselves, and if we persist in this activity–after all, why not make ourselves even better?–we must eventually transcend our original condition. In other words, during this improving process we humans will gradually transcend, as you will see, into a higher, universal kind of intelligent beings.

Summary

I have noted here two parts of us humans: our abilities and our bodies and minds. I showed why each part was chosen, and why, as a group, they cover a broad and deep span of the relevant local entities of the advancing universe. I also suggested how the continuing growth of SciTech might influence the bodies and minds of our species.

We already know that SciTech can grow forever. Now, we've selected the Seven Fundamental Abilities and our minds and bodies as the elements in ourselves that we should develop as far as possible. The next task to consider is this: can growing SciTech keep forever increasing these two parts of ourselves? If that is the case, we would find ourselves participating in an endless continuum.

If, however, the SciTech growth of the Seven Fundamental Abilities and our bodies and minds–these two parts of us–must eventually come up against insurmountable limits, i.e., maximums, then this condition would prove that our species' long progression has a natural Summit–humanity's greatest future. Since it's the maximums to the benefits of SciTech growth that prove the Summit exists, in the next chapter, let's look a little further at these maximums.

7

WHAT ARE THE FOUR KINDS OF MAXIMUMS?

This chapter was used in my first book, *Calousia: the Best Future: Let's Get There*, when I was attempting to identify our Great Progression's Summit by trying to find as many kinds of limits to our knowledge growth as possible. The focus for the present book, in contrast, is to focus on the most significant limits in each chosen category. The earlier approach has its uses, so I include it here.

There are four different kinds of maximums to the benefits from ever-growing SciTech. They are: (1) absolute, (2) non-empowering, (3) practical, and (4) Summit Beings' choice. Let's look at them in more detail. And, again, remember, it's these maximums that prove the existence of the Summit.

Absolute Maximums

Absolute maximums are those rigidly set by the universe. One example, according to present science, is the speed of light. The universe will not let any message, any massless particle, go faster than the speed of light. If future knowledge reveals that we can exceed this light speed limit, then this will simply demonstrate that we have identified the wrong speed maximum. Another absolute-maximum example is the rest mass and electric charge of an electron. Its rest mass is 0.910956×10^{-31} kilogram and its charge is $1.6021765 \times 10^{-19}$ coulomb. Future SciTech growth may increase the accuracy of these electron numbers, but it won't change them much.

The Maximums of Non-Empowering SciTech

Francis Bacon famously said; "Knowledge is power." But some SciTech doesn't empower–or at least doesn't empower very much. For example, the discovery, classification, and study of a new fossil can be wonderful science. But unless the new specimen throws a surprising new light on biological evolution or reveals unusual or useful structures, it won't significantly increase our understanding of nature or, more importantly, our capacity to control or manipulate things.

SciTech growth meets maximums in this non-empowering category because even though knowledge here may increase, it empowers only very modestly or not at all.

These first two kinds of maximums to SciTech's incessant growth and empowerment–absolute and non-empowering –depend entirely on the nature of the universe.

The next two kinds of maximums depend on the interaction between universal maximums and us ability-expanding human beings. These are practical maximums and maximums of Summit Beings' choice.

Practical Maximums

One kind of practical maximum is diminishing returns. Suppose, for example, SciTech growth somehow makes it possible to travel from New York to London in the astonishingly fast time of five minutes. Suppose also that our understanding of realities suggests that, in theory, further SciTech growth could reduce this time by 15 seconds. All considered, this potential improvement is probably not worth the effort. It's a matter of diminishing returns.

(Surprisingly, the Apollo spacecraft could travel from New York to London now in about 8.37 minutes; that is, it could fly over and between these two points in about that time. The problem is that those eight minutes don't include getting up to speed and up into space and then slowing back down and stopping. Landing at 24,790 miles per hour could be more than exciting.)

Another kind of practical maximum is where an alternative means works better. So, for example, if we're developing material for the combustion chamber of a jet engine, there's no use trying to keep improving paper for this use if other materials will always stand up to the heat better.

In this category, therefore, further growth might bring about some improvements, but producing them isn't worthwhile. This is a universal maximum because if beings like us, or superior to us, exist elsewhere in the universe, they would eventually face these diminishing returns, too.

Maximums of Summit Beings' Choice

This maximum applies when SciTech growth *could* make a particular new ability possible, but the high-capacity Summit Beings of the future (assuming they exist) would not choose to acquire it. This maximum is difficult to apply, because our present view of what these future beings will or will not want may be quite inaccurate.

Suppose, for example, the laws of genetics somehow allow the creation of mosquitoes the size of ducks. We can assume that wise Summit Beings, especially if they remain biological, will refrain from creating such creatures. Or if they do decide to produce them, it's likely they will produce only a few–say, for scientific purposes–and not let them loose in the Summit Beings' environment.

In this category, therefore, SciTech growth is maximized in the sense that its further growth can yield only unwanted abilities.

Choice by Summit Beings can be considered a universal maximum, because in light of universal laws and conditions, we can expect that these highly intelligent and informed Summit Beings will make similar rational choices under similar conditions.

We noted four kinds of maximums: absolute, practical, of non-empowering SciTech, and of Summit Beings' choice. Now, let's see how these four kinds of maximums might stop ever-growing SciTech from ever increasing various aspects of those two parts of ourselves.

As for the third part of ourselves–how we live–again, we will deal with this in a later chapter.

And again, the more maximums we find and the more important they are, the more interesting the resultant Summit future condition when all maximums are met.

You now know the four kinds of maximums to the benefits of SciTech growth, maximums that reveal the limits to the benefits of endless SciTech growth. But maximizing the two parts of us–our Seven Fundamental Abilities and our bodies and minds–is not going to be easy. In fact, these will be two of the most difficult tasks our species has ever undertaken. Why, then, undertake them? We already have too many other important chores ahead of us.

The next chapter provides the answer.

8

WHY ATTEMPT TO MAXIMIZE OUR SEVEN FUNDAMENTAL ABILITIES AND OUR BODIES AND MINDS?

If the greatest-future Summit exists, how much must we increase our Seven Fundamental Abilities and our bodies and minds in order to reveal it?

The answer, of course, is that we must increase them as much as possible, as much as universal conditions permit. In other words, we must maximize our fundamental abilities and our bodies and minds.

Why? Again, it's because these maximizations, these limits to the benefits of SciTech growth, are what produce the Summit. They are what give our species its biggest, richest, best-possible future. In other words, reaching these maximizations is crucial to our species succeeding in our self-development.

To see what this means, consider what happens if we try to maximize transportation speed. Must we learn to travel tens of thousands of miles an hour? Hundreds of thousands of miles an hour? Millions of miles an hour? If the speed of light is some 670.6 million miles an hour, does this mean we must learn to travel hundreds of millions of miles an hour?

After considering these astonishing speeds, many of you would probably think, "That's crazy!" Or, "This maximizing is an outrageously-too-big task." "It's far too difficult and costly." "It's way beyond present needs." "It's unreasonable even to start progressing that fast now." And the same could be said for maximizing both the other abilities and our bodies and minds.

And, of course, we don't yet know what this maximum travel speed is, say, to travel halfway around the Earth or from the Earth to the moon. Our present vehicles are obviously too slow for guidance, and our physical sciences suggest some limits, like traveling "x" amount slower than the speed of light, but we can't be certain now if any of these limits are ultimately correct.

On the other hand, even in our present ignorance, we can be sure that for any particular distances there must be a maximum speed, a speed no amount of additional SciTech could ever increase further. And that's the kind of maximum we are seeking here.

Another reason to maximize is that we have already begun our SciTech growth and our increase in abilities, and our abilities-expanding progression offers us no significant, logical place short of the maximums to stop. Yes, we could have stopped at the Agricultural Revolution, some 11,000 years ago, or at the Urban Revolution, some 5,000 years ago, but in each case our growing knowledge thereafter gave us essential new benefits. And SciTech growth among our fundamental abilities will continue giving us new benefits until we reach the Summit, when its benefits are at their greatest and can no longer thereafter increase, at least among the selected two parts of ourselves.

Still another reason to strive for the Summit is this: Why stop before it? Why deliberately, at some point before the Summit, give up all the other future benefits of achieving the Summit? No. The Summit benefits are too desirable to stop our advance.

Finally, we should maximize our abilities and ourselves because this maximizing is the only way we can reach our progression's true Summit, our biggest, richest, best-possible future. Reaching this Summit, in turn, is the only way that we can fulfill our species' extraordinary potential.

And remember, building a nation-wide railroad was once considered too big and costly an undertaking. The same for building an airplane, and especially one intended for commercial aviation. Similarly, hunter-gatherers would have considered villages too big and costly, rural villagers would have considered cities too big and costly, and early city dwellers would have considered today's megacities too big and costly.

But is this maximizing of ourselves just our egocentrism running amok? Sure, our egos are involved. But, as noted, completing our self-development will give our species its greatest future condition, and, as you will see, this growth makes the most of our self-advancing character. Far more important, however, as you will see in Chapter 19, is that this fulfilling of our species' extraordinary potential may well be just what the universe needs us to accomplish if the cosmos is to continue its long and amazing advance.

So, yes, this maximizing of our abilities and ourselves is an enormous and costly task. But if we keep working at it, it's doable. It's also rewarding and exciting! Moreover, it's of first importance if we want to make the most of our progressive evolution. Remember that we have been lost and, in consequence, we face an existential crisis. To save ourselves, we've got to make some big changes. What better changes could we make than those that can help us succeed in our species' Great Progression?

And one more reason for maximizing: We tend to be habituated to the present state of our advance as though this is all there is, this is all we can be. We are caterpillars and that's all we'll ever be. This point of view retards our advance and keeps our "world" small. To succeed, we must allow ourselves to think bigger, to think outside our chrysalis. We must consider our self-improving, abilities-expanding character. We must, as difficult and unrealistic as this task seems, even consider a possible universal-scale role for ourselves.

For example, we know that the progressing universe consists of some two trillion other galaxies. Amid all these galaxies, how many other ability-expander groups like us humans do you suppose the universe has created? So far, we know of none. But if it turns out that the universe has created one or more other ability-expander groups, which statistically seems certain, then we are inescapably in an evolutionary competition with these extraterrestrial beings. It's to see, who among us has what it takes to succeed in fully reaching our Great Progression's Summit. This means we must fully complete our self-developing progression. If none of us succeeds—which in such a huge task is possible—then the universe's long advance will be prematurely blocked. Furthermore, the fewer the number of existing ability-expanding groups there are, the greater the significance of those who ultimately succeed.

So, yes, this task of maximizing is certainly unusual and difficult for us, and it may at first seem excessive, but I hope the above points help you understand why this maximizing of our Seven Fundamental Abilities and our bodies and minds is essential.

In sum, why should we maximize our fundamental abilities and ourselves? **First**, because the more we increase our abilities, the greater our benefits. **Second**, because there's no logical place short of the maximums to stop. **Third**, because if we stop at some point before the Summit, this action would deprive us of all the remaining great advantages to be enjoyed at the Summit. **Fourth,** because this maximizing is the only way we can reach our progression's true Summit, and enjoy our biggest, richest, best-possible future. **Fifth,** because reaching this Summit is the only way that we can fulfill our species' extraordinary potential. **Sixth**, because, as you will see, reaching the Summit is the way we help our advancing universe progress locally. **Seventh**, because presumably we are in a kind of competition with all the other ability expanders around the universe, assuming they exist, and we don't want to be found lagging, to be unable to fulfill our assigned role in the advancing universe. And, **eighth**, because this is the way to understand our species' astonishing purpose.

But is it possible to maximize our Seven Fundamental Abilities? And if it's possible, how do we do it? That's the topic of the next chapter.

9

HOW SHOULD WE MAXIMIZE OUR SEVEN FUNDAMENTAL ABILITIES?

Our purpose here is to prove that our species' long abilities-expanding evolution, our Great Progression, that biggest and most important achievement of our species, has a Summit, a dazzling, natural, specific, greatest-future Summit. So far, the existence of a Summit has seemed impossible. This is because the growth of SciTech itself, the primary driver of our progression, appears endless.

What conditions would characterize a Summit of our great abilities-expanding progression? Two things. It's when our growing SciTech has expanded both our Seven Fundamental Abilities and our bodies and minds as far as possible. In other words, it's when these two categories that make up ourselves become maximized or virtually maximized. Thereafter, SciTech growth can never increase these two parts of us further. That's why the resulting condition is a distinctive high point, a Summit. Again, as noted, the third part of us–how we live–will be considered later. So the purpose of this chapter and the next is to find significant areas where growing SciTech maximizes both the Seven Fundamental Abilities and our bodies and minds.

In my previous book, I gave a long chapter to each of the fundamental abilities and the same to the changes in ourselves. I tried to find every maximum I could. And each of these two areas tend to be broad and complex.

In the paragraphs below, I will try to reduce this complexity by focusing on the most important subject in each area that can be maximized. In other words, I think that using this group of these most important maximums in each area is really sufficient to identify the Summit.

Note that this approach comes with a rough assumption. It assumes that those who succeed in growing their SciTech until they maximize this brief Summit example, will have also acquired, or will soon, the additional SciTech, techniques, tools, and knowledge necessary to maximize the other maximizable parts of that category.

So let's see if important aspects of the Seven Fundamental Abilities and our bodies and minds can be maximized and so prove that our species' long Great Progression has a natural, highly-desirable Summit. Let's start in our species' elemental realm.

Maximizing Our Seven Fundamental Abilities

1. The Elemental Realm

We will determine maximums in this realm by synthesis. In this case, it's the ability to synthesize the entities of this realm accurately, rapidly, and efficiently. Since this elemental realm is enormous and since we are just beginning our proofs of maximums, i.e., limits to the benefits of growing SciTech, we will focus here on this realm's smaller entities, meaning finding maximums to the synthesis of atoms, inorganic molecules, minerals, and organic molecules.

Regarding **atoms**, the Periodic Table lists 118 kinds of atoms, called elements. For simplicity, let's choose the 90 stable kinds of elements naturally found on Earth. We would meet the maximums in this category when growing SciTech allows us to make, fast and efficiently, a thimbleful of each of these 90 kinds of elements from the most difficult source: energy. Synthesis of all larger entities in this realm can thereafter be made from atoms that are easier to obtain.

Regarding **inorganic molecules**, we choose 50 examples representative of all inorganic molecules from a synthesis point of view. Once growing SciTech allows us to create the appropriate automatic analyzing devices and molecular synthesizing machines that can synthesize half a measuring cup of each of these chosen fifty kinds of inorganic molecules as accurately, quickly, and efficiently as possible, we would reach the maximums here, reach the limits to growing SciTech's benefits for producing these fifty.

Again, once we have accomplished this task, with only a little extra SciTech growth, we can soon use these same kinds of analyzing and synthesis machines to analyze and synthesize virtually all the other inorganic molecules. So we will have established the maximums here for the entire inorganic molecular group.

Regarding **minerals,** some 5,500 different kinds are known. As above, we select 200 minerals that are representative of the entire mineral group from a synthesis point of view. And, again, when growing SciTech allows us to create automatic analyzing and synthesizing devices that can synthesize a half cup of each of all these 200 chosen examples as accurately, quickly, and efficiently as possible, we would not only maximize these 200, but we would know we could soon maximize the synthesis of any of all the other thousands of minerals.

About **organic molecules,** many millions of kinds are known, but growing SciTech will also allow us to create more complex organic analyzing and synthesizing devices. Again we select 200 organic molecules as closely representative of this entire category as we can and synthesize a half cup of each of them as accurately, rapidly, and efficiently as possible. This process tells us we have the knowledge and tools that would allow us to soon synthesize to the maximum any of the other millions of organic molecules to the maximum.

What if another set of analyzing and synthesizing machines can produce these entities faster, more accurately, and efficiently? Then these new devices would constitute the new maximum. Or, the difference between them isn't great enough to matter.

It is in this way that we demonstrate the maximums, show the limits to the benefits of growing SciTech, for the smaller entities of this elemental category.

Most important, note that these automatic devices could not only copy all these various kinds of inorganic and organic molecules and minerals, but they could also be used to soon create virtually any possible and advantageous new kinds of molecules and minerals we wanted. This category of elemental synthesis also encompasses a vast number of larger structures—paper clips, scissors, silicon chips, computers, electric automobiles, etc. But the above portion is a reasonable start.

2. The Biological Realm

Maximizing in this large and very complex realm is again demonstrated by synthesis, an imperfect but reasonably good proof of maximizing. We must first select 60 species, ten from each of the six major biological kingdoms that together are roughly representative of all kingdoms from a synthesis point of view. (The six categories are archaebacteria, eubacteria, fungi, protista, plants, and animals.) Then, after learning to create the appropriate analyzing and synthesizing devices, we must synthesize accurately, rapidly, and efficiently, from on-the-shelf chemicals, good living copies of all 60 species.

This means we would soon acquire the capacity to create living copies of all the single celled species. Of the multicellular species, it means creating the living fertilized cells from on-the-shelf chemicals and nurturing them to their species' maturity. Once we had accomplished this for these 60 representative species, we would know that our SciTech had grown enough to give us sufficient knowledge, tools, and techniques to soon make accurate living copies of any other earthly species.

We should perform another procedure here. First, we should select a few typical multicellular examples of the biological realm. Then, among each of these we should determine exactly how the same DNA in the fertilized egg of each of these example species, DNA that is repeated in virtually all subsequent cells of the organism, can appropriately produce all the different specialized cells, tissues, organs, and systems, when and wherever needed, in the mature specimen.

Finally, we must also understand how to use biology's genetic system, perhaps greatly changed, to produce new kinds of substances and materials, and perhaps even to store knowledge.

As noted, when our growing SciTech finally gives us the knowledge, tools, and techniques to perform the above tasks, this synthesis capacity would mark the practical summit of biology. This knowledge doesn't tell how all these different organisms live. It doesn't explain their ecosystems. But it's good enough for present purposes. And those who have acquired this impressive synthesis capacity could undoubtedly soon acquire particulars about these other areas of biology as well.

3. The Astronomical Realm

We find the maximums here when our SciTech growth finally produces the knowledge, techniques, and tools to create **mastery in two areas**.

The first is a general universal history. We must understand how the universe originated, how it has changed since its birth, and what we can expect of it as far as it exists into the distant future.

The second area starts with a catalogue of the universe's important components. Then we must learn how each of these components typically begins, lives, and dies, both when it is isolated and when it is influenced by other components of its environment. Yes, we can expect our growing SciTech thereafter will reveal new, quite unusual phenomena, but these new examples will not materially change this general astronomical view. In other words, this astronomical ability is maximizable.

4. Communication

Communication has four important aspects: message speed, density, cost, and accessibility. I'll focus here on message speed. It's the most important of these four parts of communication because, along with transportation, these two factors determine the size of the sphere within the universe that we can practically manage in a reasonable length of time. The message itself might be spoken, written, printed, or computer generated.

Message speed has one of three possible maximums: (1) light speed, (2) some particular greater speed, and (3) no speed limit. According to **Albert Einstein's** special theory of relativity, no message can travel faster than the speed of light, the speed of massless photons in a vacuum, which is about 300,000 kilometers or 186,000 miles per second. If Einstein is right, then the universe sets strict maximums to this aspect of communication. Once growing SciTech permits the sending of messages at light speed, no additional SciTech can ever increase it further. And, of course, with radio we attained this speed some time ago.

Most scientists today would choose light speed as the communication maximum, except for the existence of entangled particles. In theory, if one of an entangled pair of particles rests here on Earth and the other lies 4.3 light-years away at the nearest star, and you examine one of them, the other will instantly change. So speculations about faster-than-light communication are not entirely absurd.

If the universe does allow faster-than-light communication, can we find the maximums now? Yes. Strangely, we can. We know that any faster means must be one of two kinds: the universe either sets limits to this faster speed or it doesn't. If it limits speed to some particular faster-than-light rate—say, 10 or 10,000 times faster—or to some special manipulations, then the unsurpassable universal limit, the maximum, is just this greater speed or the shorter time due to the special manipulations.

In the improbable case that the universe sets no communication speed limit, then messages could be sent anywhere in the universe instantly.

We cannot be absolutely sure now which of the three possible speed maximums is the true one. But we know the maximum must be one of them, and that suffices for now.

I also found maximums to the three other less important aspects of communication. So once we reach these additional maximums, no further growth of SciTech or increase in intelligence (human or nonhuman) could expand these abilities further. No one could send more bits per second over a channel. No one could transmit messages at a lower energy cost. And no one could access the communication system better. In sum, the fundamental ability of communication can be maximized.

But wait! There is a fifth, very important aspect of communication not yet considered. It's the information being transmitted. The maximum here is that every Summit Being should have virtually immediate access to every part of all acquired Summit knowledge delivered electronically, to their computers, or through speech, writing, pictures, and movies. This system would be like an advanced Google. What is the natural limit here? It's not to knowledge acquisition, which is limitless. It's when SciTech growth finally creates the relevant equipment for the storage, access, and delivery of all this information. We are making good progress there now.

5. Transportation

The key aspect of transportation is also speed. Therefore, we must first select, say, just five destinations distant enough from each other to require quite different transportation means. I chose: (a) ten miles away; (b) 500 miles away; (c) halfway around the world; (d) the distance from Earth to the far reaches of the solar system, perhaps to Jupiter's moon Europa; and (e) from Earth to one of the planets orbiting the nearest stars, perhaps to a habitable planet, Proxima b, orbiting the star Proxima Centauri. Then we must learn to travel as fast as possible to each of these five destinations–which could be hundreds of millions of mph. Completing this task would maximize travel speed, because we would know we could soon travel as fast as possible to anywhere else within this entire area.

Another shorter possible measure of the transportation maximum might be this: to learn to travel as fast as possible, for a week (or perhaps a specific longer period) through space. The assumption here is that those with the SciTech tools, knowledge, and techniques to build the power devices and vehicles just mentioned probably have also acquired, or will soon, the ability to reach the maximums in other transportation tasks–such as the specific distances noted above or the fastest travel over land or water.

6. Access to Energy

A ten pound goose flies through our open window, breaks its neck hitting the wall, and drops dead on the mantel. Badly needing energy, we attempt to get it from this unexpected arial source. Since the bird is still warm, we try for its heat energy. We drop it to the floor for its gravitational energy. We separate its atoms and molecules to get its chemical energy. And when it's dry, we burn it to get more of its heat energy. Despite our best efforts, this creature turns out to be a foul energy source.

But wait. We can tap this bird's mass energy. **Isaac Asimov** tells us that getting all ten pounds of this goose's mass energy would give us the same energy as burning nine million tons of gasoline. Our energy problems are solved!

Although energy exists in an awesome number of different forms, this goose example shows there's no need for a similarly large number of means to tap each form. To maximize energy, to find the limits in this realm to the benefits of growing SciTech, we must perform just three tasks: first, identify the largest energy sources; next, find the low number of practical and efficient means to tap these sources; and finally, improve these methods as much as possible. This would provide the abundance of energy we assume Summit Beings enjoy.

7. Power Devices

Focus here on two kinds of power devices, engines (driven by chemical power, such as gasoline or rocket fuel) and motors (driven by the electromagnetic force). These two devices dominate motion-producing devices now and will undoubtedly continue to be important in the future. In addition, we know that the designs and materials of each kind of engine or motor can be altered in innumerable ways for special purposes, conditions, sizes, etc. But here, we will consider only the basic engine and motor designs.

We have already developed many such devices and, as we progress, we will undoubtedly create many more. We nevertheless find limits, and therefore maximizations, with respect to how much ever-growing SciTech can practically keep improving basic engine and motor designs in the following five areas: Maximums due to (1) the low number of basic principles that transform energy in some form into kinetic energy; (2) limits due to the character of the type of energy used; (3) the limited basic designs that can efficiently tap this energy; (4) limits on appropriate materials; and (5) limits on improvement.

Once growing SciTech produces the basic engine and motor designs that best meet the demands of the above five categories, it will maximize this power device category.

I have noted the preponderance of limits, or maximizations, among the Seven Fundamental Abilities. This is a potent, dominating, broad, deep, and fundamental group of technical achievements. It's important to say again that once these fundamental abilities have been maximized, none of them can ever be increased thereafter, no matter how much either SciTech or intelligence (human or nonhuman) should grow.

These maximized Seven Fundamental Abilities are one part of ourselves. But, of course, there's another part of us humans that we must maximize to reach the Summit: our bodies and our minds. Is it possible to maximize this difficult area? The next chapter explains.

10

HOW SHOULD WE MAXIMIZE OUR BODIES AND MINDS? HUMAN SELF-REALIZATION. OUR POTENTIAL-FILLING PROGRESSION

In Chapter Two, we explored what we humans are. We saw that we have traditionally characterized ourselves as wise, tool users, and culture bearers. We saw that this rather static characterization of ourselves is inappropriate and dangerous. It is inappropriate because it misses our species' most important and unique characteristic, namely, our ability to grow in knowledge and capability, which has continually changed how we live. In other words, traditionally, we haven't **really understood what we humans are**. And this, of course, is a crucial part of identifying our species greatest future.

This old characterization of us–wise, tool users, etc.–was dangerous because it tended to keep us from understanding ourselves. It tended to keep us unaware that as our knowledge grew, our abilities, and our bodies and minds too, would keep expanding, a consequence of our continually growing knowledge of biology, genetics, robotics, and artificial intelligence.

Here, in the maximizing of our bodies and minds, we must come to terms with the changes that our growing knowledge must make in us.

We must now find that we are not just ability expanders. We must awaken in ourselves our understanding that our great progression reveals that we are primarily a self-developing species. In time, as our knowledge naturally grows, we will become a self-transforming species and eventually a self-transcending species.

This self-transformation is just the natural progression of our self-developing character, the continuation of our growth of abilities, especially in biology and genetics, and the resulting changes in how we live. Yes, we will now be moving in ways we've never attempted before. But we must confidently move beyond that old, static, dangerous, inhibiting characterization of ourselves, and awaken to the extraordinary benefits of our natural, expansive self-development.

So let's start exploring our astonishing, natural, future growth now.

We humans are remarkable, unique beings, the only species on Earth that can keep improving itself through knowledge growth. But we humans are not yet completed beings, not yet developed to our full potential. This completion of ourselves into our mature universal form is a major part of our species' self-developing, self-creating goal.

How do universal Summit Beings' bodies and minds differ from those of us human ability-expanders today? We don't know. We have no models. We've never seen a true

Summit Being. We've never even seen other extra terrestrial ability expanders like ourselves. In consequence, we don't know if our present human ability-expander bodies and minds are a highly advanced example of our universal type or a very primitive example. Similarly, we have no idea how far we must change ourselves to become Summit Beings, assuming such beings exist elsewhere.

We should be prepared, however, to accept the real possibility that our bodies and minds at the Summit will differ enormously from those we have now.

But why attempt to maximize our bodies and minds?

1. Obviously, this task is most unusual. We've never attempted it before. We haven't even seriously considered it before. We have no models. We don't know what we're doing in this strange new area; so we are quite unprepared for this task.

2. Note that our bodies and minds are pretty good already. We can do an astonishing number of different things: climb cliffs, dance ballet, play football, thread needles, care for our bodies, read and understand an encyclopedia, remember important things, create new ideas and new tools, manipulate single atoms, level great hills, the list goes on.

3. But we aren't perfect. We remain animals, mammals. We suffer from mutations, get sick, are injured. Our minds are good, but they could be better. In fact, we already know there are people among us now whose minds work in certain ways much better than our own, people who are better at: learning, remembering, forgetting, focusing, discerning, inventing, creating, reasoning, accessing

information, drawing conclusions from what's known and unknown, being sensitive, and on and on.

4. As with the seven fundamental abilities, if there are maximums to the development of our bodies and minds, then there is no logical place for us, in our self-developing progression, to stop short of reaching these maximums.

5. We are by our natures a self-improving species, so it's appropriate for us to make the most of ourselves, if we can.

6. Most important, if it's possible to be far more capable beings than we presently are, we should start exploring this subject now, get started now, so we can become and enjoy being these improved beings sooner.

7. Also, consider the caterpillar-butterfly interaction. If we don't know how amazingly better we can be, then it's obvious, as noted before, that we don't know what we humans really are. Our ignorance here, our long tradition here, holds us back, and keeps us from being the most we can be.

Conclusion: We should seriously consider the improvement and, eventually, the maximization, of our bodies and minds.

As we attempt to maximize our bodies and minds or even improve them, here are **three important preliminary topics to consider.**

The **first** concerns **management.** How should we commence our future self-transformation? Should we organize and manage this task as we have other giant tasks? Or should we proceed as we usually have, letting interested individuals and institutions around the world independently work on whatever parts of this task interest them, and leaving the rest to chance?

The answer is that this task is far too important to all humans and to our future to continue with our disorganized approach. We just can't mess this task up. We cannot just let individuals around the globe–rank amateurs as well as experts–make inheritable changes in our species, some of them good, many of them disfiguring, painful, and life-destroying. Such a crucial subject must be managed by one authorized, world wide organization, operating openly. Since humans are already fast advancing in learning to make deliberate genetic changes, we must create this organization in the very near future.

The **second** preliminary subject concerns **specialization.** We humans perform, and need to perform, hundreds of different kinds of tasks every day. Think of all the little things we do without much thought: reach for a toothbrush, find the toothpaste and put it on the brush, brush our teeth, turn the water on and off, find and put on our shoes, perhaps tie shoe laces, walk, run, climb, get into a vehicle, drive, follow road rules, and so on.

As we improve ourselves, we must be careful not to become so specialized that we can't do all the many kinds of tasks that we have always done and all those additional necessary and desirable tasks waiting for us in the future. In other words, as we improve ourselves, we must be very careful to remain unspecialized Calousian beings and to use specialized tools for specialized tasks.

The **third** preliminary subject to consider as we think of improving ourselves in the future concerns **environments,** particularly extra terrestrial ones. This is because environments will obviously influence body choices. For example, stronger gravities will require heavier, stronger legs; light gravities could allow us to be thinner and taller.

Some future environments will lack oxygen, have poisonous air, offer greater extremes of temperature than found on Earth, and might be unable to support the growth of the plants and animals that we now use for food.

We have built space stations, and we will soon have colonies on the moon and on Mars, places with different gravities, and where natural air, food, and water are rare or absent.

One response to difficult environments is that, instead of changing our bodies, we do what we do in different environments on Earth and in space; namely, we wear appropriate clothing and create comfortable mini environments like houses and larger structures. And we can expect that Summit Beings, with their superior abilities, will be able to create these necessary alterations of apparel and housing far better than we can.

The other response to difficult environments is to change them to better suit us, for example, to terraform them, as we have thought of changing Mars.

Since Summit Beings will undoubtedly inhabit many different kinds of environments, and therefore maximize themselves in very different ways, how can we appropriately simplify this part of our body-maximizing problem?

The answer is to select three very different environments and then maximize our bodies for each. The **first** of these three environments can be Earth, with all its many micro-environments, which we are already well adapted to. The **second** is the extremely different environment of space—e.g., a huge spaceship or a very tiny moon—with zero gravity, no oxygen, and only the materials we brought with us or those at the minimal site to work with. Think how different our bodies must therefore be and how much our SciTech must grow to provide all those accessing and recycling needs. The **third** environment might be of an opposite kind to Earth, a much heavier planet and perhaps closer to its star or our sun.

The first changes, of course, should be altering our clothing, habitations, and environments to better suit us as we have done on Earth. But the other two environments are so different from Earth's that successful living there will require altering ourselves, too. And to fulfill our potential, we must learn how to do that and do it well. My assumption is that beings smart enough to accomplish these tasks in these three, very different environments would also be informed enough to soon adjust themselves reasonably well to any other additional possible desired environments.

Why bother adapting our bodies to these two other very different environments? So far, we have needed to adjust ourselves only to earthly conditions. But just as in our past, when we adjusted first and only to Africa, and then spread around the globe to its very different environments, so in our future, after adjusting only to earthly conditions, we can expect to spread to very different environments far from our planet of origin. And we should know what changes in us are essential for this effort to be successful.

The basic idea here is that by growing SciTech enough to create Summit Beings' bodies and minds for these three quite different environments, we can maximize ourselves.

How should we begin this transformation of us humans into Summit Beings?

The necessary initial step in improving ourselves should be to **better understand our present bodies and minds.**

Scientists have now created three new tools essential to this effort.

The **first** is **sequencing machines**, which allow us to precisely identify the sequence of the four molecular nucleic acid components of our inherited DNA molecule, a molecule that exists in virtually every cell of our bodies. Without this DNA knowledge we couldn't really know what genes are or why they work the way they do.

The **second** essential new tool is the **global Human Cell Atlas.** Its purpose is to identify and map every cell type in the human body, which contains some 37 trillion cells. In other words, it will tell us, for the first time, what we humans really are. This is obviously basic, essential knowledge if we want to improve ourselves.

The **third** tool is the **CRISPR** technology that will allow us to correct dangerous mutations in our DNA and, in the future, give us new and better genes. If you plan a child, sequencing machines can identify serious mutations in the genes of you and your spouse, and remove them at the conception of your child.

Synthesizing Copies of Individual Humans

Before we alter ourselves, however, we should know ourselves better, and a proof of this is the ability to make good copies of individual humans. We will maximize this area when we can perform the following **six manipulations** as quickly and efficiently as possible.

The **first** manipulation is the analysis of the reproductive cells of two chosen humans, a man and a woman, and then the synthesis, from on-the-shelf chemicals, of a true copy of their fertilized eggs.

The **second** manipulation is the above procedure with twelve males and twelve females representative of humanity. The **third** manipulation, from parents wanting the resulting babies, is to succeed in raising their twelve individual fertilized eggs to live birth weight. The **fourth** is the synthesis of representative human body parts from single cells.

The **fifth** task is to understand how the single fertilized egg, with its distinctive DNA, multiplies this same DNA in every cell and alters access to various parts of the DNA molecule to create all the many kinds of cells and structures of the mature individual's body. As for the brain, we must understand how its cells multiply and specialize in interaction with their individual environments from the earliest stages to birth, and then from birth to full maturity. In addition, we must learn what the different parts of the brain do, how they do it, and how they interact to produce the activities of a living brain, such as learning, memory, appropriate forgetting, thought, judgments, purpose, sensations, and consciousness.

Once we have maximized these five tasks, performed them as efficiently as possible, we will know that we can create, from on-the-shelf chemicals, **a good living copy of any human**.

Once we acquire the above noted knowledge to better understand our bodies and minds, how should we begin to improve these two parts of ourselves?

First, remember our **maximizing purpose** here. It's not to become a better animal, mammal, or *Homo sapiens*. It's not, as noted earlier, just to make the best of what we are.

It's to transcend into Summit Beings, the higher kind of beings that mark the universal Summit of our species' long progressive advance.

So what then is our species' Great Progression? The answer is that it's our species' Great, Self-Transcending Progression.

One obvious early task is to begin correcting **harmful mutations**. We could do this, first, at conception. As noted, we are just starting to do this now. Then we might begin correcting these mutations later in young or adult individuals.

We should also begin to identify **additional genetic changes** that might be appropriate. The more our SciTech grows, the more evident are the improvements possible in ourselves. Furthermore, it's reasonable to expect that when our growing SciTech allows us to make true improvements to our bodies and minds, we will make them.

We could certainly identify obviously **advantageous genes in particular individuals**. These genes might then be duplicated and inserted into the genomes of a few selected fertilized human eggs, to determine if these new genes continue to be clearly advantageous when transferred to others. If they pass this test, these new genes could eventually be made available for all new conceptions.

Regarding our **senses**, we must thoroughly understand our seven kinds: touch, hearing, taste, smell, sight, heat, and our body's position. Then we must examine the senses of humans and animals that are different and better than ours. In hearing, we must consider a wider range of air vibrations, and in sight, explore wider areas of the electromagnetic spectrum. We must examine a wider range of tastes and smells, too. Eventually, we must decide how much of all these and other sensory areas are important enough to include in our unspecialized bodies, leaving access to the rest of the desired senses to tools.

Regarding our **minds**, we are already learning more about AI, artificial intelligence, for example, to produce self-driving cars. Creating ever better artificial minds will enormously help us understand our own minds and reveal possible improvements.

Eventually, we must find ways to vastly improve learning and forgetting, so we can learn much faster and remember what we want more accurately and also forget all that should be forgotten. Our minds might also be altered so that we can concentrate more effectively when that's needed, and can let our thoughts run in various directions at times when that's helpful. Our minds might also be made more creative when this faculty is desired. Also, we must find ways for injured minds to be quickly and easily repaired. It would be helpful, too, if minds had an automatic logic check, to alert us against believing two conflicting facts or ideas at the same time. It's important, too, that we keep improving access to the planet wide Web with its massive quantity of high quality data, so that almost any wanted facts can rapidly be accessed.

But can our human bodies and minds be maximized?

Note that if we truly maximize our Seven Fundamental Abilities at the Summit, they **cannot thereafter be increased.** However, if we maximize our bodies and minds, it's reasonable that we may well desire to make changes in ourselves after becoming Summit Beings: for different environments, for different purposes, or just out of the desire for change. Therefore, let's consider bodies and minds at the Summit as being **virtually maximized**. That's good enough for now.

So, again, can our human bodies and minds be virtually maximized?

Note that advancing some part of our bodies and minds often has a cost to other advantageous abilities. For example, making our hands stronger can be valuable for some tasks, such as lifting heavy boulders, but it also makes them less able to do delicate, little tasks well, such as threading a tiny needle. And remember that we want to remain generalized beings and to use specialized tools for specialized tasks.

Let us assume, as seems reasonable, that if we grow SciTech until we maximize our Seven Fundamental Abilities and keep improving our general sensory, bodily, and mental characteristics, and continue exploring many options, we must eventually become so improved for our three chosen environments that growing SciTech thereafter cannot significantly improve us further. This is because the high-capacity SciTech, already accumulated, would, on our first reaching the Summit, allow us to then make any of those desired future additional changes we desire.

When do we virtually maximize our bodies and minds?

It's when, for our three environments, we make in ourselves all the possible, highly desirable advanced improvements that do not seriously diminish the other highly desirable advanced parts of us.

What will we be like when we have maximized ourselves into Summit Beings?

We can't really know now, but we can make some educated guesses.

Would we remain **mammals**? That is certainly our history and probably our preference. But it's doubtful. We can't expect other Summit Beings around the universe to be true mammals as we are. Furthermore, the mammal choice means we would be little changed at the Summit, not advancing far enough to fulfill our extraordinary potential. We might give ourselves such mammalian characteristics as warm bodies, loving natures, and the long nurturing of our young, however.

Would we remain **animals**? Each adult human is like a mega-city, an organized collection of some 37 trillion individual living cells of different kinds organized into systems that perform specific functions. These living parts of us ever need us for their food and drink, and ever cause us to get rid of their waste. Yes, remaining animals is a possibility. But aren't we really unnecessarily complex and difficult to maintain and improve?

There's another possibility. Our **robots** with artificial intelligence are becoming ever smarter and more capable. Eventually, their bodies and minds may become far superior to ours. Our choice, then, may be either to greatly improve ourselves to keep up with them, or to adopt their character and become ultra-superior "robots" ourselves.

Robot is a terrible term in this context because of its implied great inferiority to humans. What we may become are living, conscious, socially-created and socially-assembled nonbiological beings, rather than biological, animal beings created by particular animal couples. We could have all the advantages we have now and many, many more as well. This choice would also free us of bacterial and viral diseases, cancers, long term illnesses, long and severe pain, and make us easily and quickly repairable, as it will be possible to simply replace any injured or defective parts. I'm not predicting or advancing this kind of future. I'm saying that it's a possible choice we might make as our knowledge grows and as we seek to maximize ourselves.

Would our societies then consist of many classes of assembled beings and humans? Possibly, but for me it's far preferable to have just one class.

Summit Beings may choose to **look different** from one another and from less advanced beings. However, with their maximized Seven Fundamental Abilities, their virtually maximized bodies and minds, and the way they look, live, and behave, Summit Beings should be readily distinguished from all the less advanced ability expanders and as essentially equal to all other Summit Beings, no matter how much further these more advanced beings may progress. To clarify this latter point, consider physically mature humans, say, 21 year olds. They can change and grow after reaching their maturity, but are still considered humans, so Summit Beings, too, can change and grow after reaching the Summit, yet all still be considered Summit Beings. And this, of course is a crucial part of our species' new astonishing purpose. It takes so much knowledge and so many abilities and techniques to become Summit Beings that any particular further bodily and mental changes they make in the future could soon have also been made shortly after becoming Summit Beings.

As noted in the previous chapter, to master this biological realm, we must also know how to efficiently use biology's genetic system, perhaps greatly altered, for new uses, such as for making desirable substances and materials and perhaps for storing information.

I've now shown how maximizations of the Seven Fundamental Abilities and the virtual maximization of our bodies and minds determine the Summit to our species' abilities-expanding evolution, our Great Progression. Note, however, that the Summit is also characterized by much other knowledge and many other kinds of maximizations. Let's now explore these ideas.

11

MAXIMIZING BEYOND OUR SEVEN FUNDAMENTAL ABILITIES AND OUR BODIES AND MINDS

You now understand how to maximize the Seven Fundamental Abilities and Our Bodies and Minds, the two parts of us. It's worth noting, however, that our progression's Summit is also characterized by its knowledge in four other areas.

1. All the enabling knowledge acquired

Another reason the maximizing of the two parts of us amounts to a Summit condition is all the additional knowledge that must be acquired to get there. Think, for example, of all the scientific, technological, mathematical, and engineering knowledge necessary to create the required tools, materials, theories, and procedures to reach the maximums. Think of all the chemical and physical knowledge that lets us build rocket ships, computer chips, DNA sequencing machines, communication satellites, and accelerators with their complex detectors. In sum, we reach maximums among the two parts of us only as a consequence of having acquired an enormous body of sophisticated additional knowledge.

2. Maximums among abilities that cannot be maximized

So far, we have focused on the maximums of maximizable fundamental abilities, for example, a human can go without air for only so long. Let's now consider maximums among un-maximizable abilities, in other words, those abilities that seem to have no limit.

We can assume that those who acquire the former, being curious and technically adept, will also have explored the most important of the latter, the un-maximizable abilities, and found many limits there as well.

For example, in the realm of biological synthesis, consider how each species might be varied. The possibilities are truly infinite. Nevertheless, even here the limits of diminishing returns and Summit Beings' choice could apply. Take chickens, for example. By the time we humans reach the Summit Beings' level of knowledge, we likely will have had an opportunity to create, or computer model, a great many varieties of chickens. And of these, we humans will have selected all those significant to the Summit Beings' way of life, assuming some varieties meet these criteria. So although it's possible to create an infinite variety of kinds of chickens, and possible that many may be produced in small quantities, we can expect that those humans nearing Summit capacity must reach a point where there's little benefit, the environment being constant, to creating further varieties of these birds, particularly if Summit Beings don't eat meat. So this is a case in which practical maximums would be met even in an infinite category. We can expect to find an enormous number of such categories and maximums.

3. Natural maximums to non-fundamental abilities

To give you some idea of the great size of this category, consider some aspects of your daily routine. For example, there's a limit, a maximum speed at which you can take a shower to shift from a particular level of dirtiness to a particular level of cleanliness. There's a practical maximum, omitting perfumes, to how much your soap can be improved for cleaning dirt from your body. There's also a maximum to how fast you can brush your teeth to a certain level of cleanliness, and another to how fast you can comb your hair from a particular ruffled state to a particular combed state.

You face practical maximums, too, to how much just the cleaning aspect of your toothpaste can practically be improved for the condition of your teeth and mouth. There's a maximum to how fast you can fry your breakfast eggs. And there's a maximum to how fast you can get two eggs from their dish and fully into your mouth (not at once, of course). There is also a maximum to how fast your egg dish can be cleaned from a particular level of dirtiness to a given level of cleanliness. Finally, whether you walk or drive to work, there's a maximum to how fast you can get from your front door to and through your office door, assuming you have an office.

My detailing of all these silly maximums in just a few of our daily activities may lack elegance and precision, but it clearly suggests that by the time we reach the Summit, we will have encountered maximums, if we want to, to an enormous number of other activities and abilities.

4. All the other knowledge acquired

A further reason that the maximized two parts of ourselves provide a Summit condition is because of all the additional unrelated knowledge acquired along the way, not only in SciTech but in many other areas as well.

As for the SciTech portion, consider that by the time people have reached our progression's Summit, all people will know about the evolution of the universe, the condition of local and distant planets, geology, ecology, local means of transportation, and all the medical technology to detect and cure illness and keep us healthy.

As for other areas of knowledge, think of what will be known of law, governance, art, literature, astronomy, education, economics, social science, language, architecture, urban design, and materials for homes and clothing. Think also of what will be known of technology-expanders, on Earth and elsewhere, and about high-tech entertainment such as three-dimensional games and virtual reality.

Add to this the point, made in Chapter Four, that SciTech is the basis for virtually all other activities. It lies behind the arts and humanities, behind our work and leisure pursuits. It chiefly determines the structure of society, strongly influences how we interact with others, and in the future will even physically influence our bodies and minds.

In conclusion, the Summit Beings' knowledge includes the maximization of the Seven Fundamental Abilities and the virtual maximization of our human bodies and minds; therefore it includes the fact that so many of these abilities and conditions cannot thereafter be increased. It also includes all the additional SciTech knowledge that lets us reach all those maximums, together with the maximums among the un-maximizable fundamental technologies, the maximums among other abilities, and all the other knowledge acquired.

Summary

The acquisition of all this maximized knowledge produces **a distinctive future Summit condition**. So yes, if we can keep growing our SciTech, keep expanding our abilities and ourselves, we can certainly know where our progressive, accelerating process should take us. It's to the Summit, which I will discuss below.

Furthermore, if ability-expanding beings like us humans arise elsewhere in the universe–which seems likely, since there are some two trillion galaxies–they would grow SciTech because it is useful and because they can; and if they keep growing it, they must eventually meet the same maximums, and the same virtual maximums, that we humans will meet, and they will therefore reach the same brilliant universal Summit condition that we face.

So where are we? I have shown why the Seven Fundamental Abilities and our bodies and minds are important and that they can be maximized or virtually maximized. This proves what I set out to prove; namely, that **our species' long growth of abilities has a natural greatest-future Summit.**

It must be emphasized that those who reach all these maximums would not know everything. But reaching all the maximums to those Seven Fundamental Abilities and bodies and minds, those two parts of us, would give these Summit Beings an enormous range and depth of knowledge that growing SciTech could never thereafter increase. Furthermore, the knowledge, tools, materials, and techniques acquired by then would give these future beings such a mastery over the analysis and synthesis of items of the components of our "world" that they could soon produce virtually any possible entity.

A List of Important Definitions

So what should we call our future maximized or near-maximized Summit Beings? To find the answer, I contacted a professor of Classical Greek language at UC Berkeley. After hearing details of this biggest, richest, best-possible future, he suggested that I call this Summit "Calousia" (Kah-lou'-see-ah), from two classical Greek words "kalos" and "ousia" meaning "beautiful existence." I liked its meaning and sound. It seemed something well worth striving for. "Calousians" (Kah-lou'-see-ahns), then, are the primary individual members of a Calousia. From now on I will use **"Calousia"** as synonymous with **"Summit"** and **"Calousians"** as synonymous with **"Summit Beings."**

Note that **Calousia is a system** consisting of Calousian individuals, their society, their territory, and all the material entities associated with them. When considering more than one such example of this advanced state that may exist through the universe, I call them "Calousian systems" or "**Calousias**."

Since our abilities-expanding evolution makes us naturally inclined to transform ourselves at the Summit into Calousians, it makes sense to call this entire process "Calousian Creation Evolution" or, for short, just **Calousian Creation**.

This **definition, of course, is universal**. Calousia is that part of the Advancing Universe (AU) in which the self-developing, abilities-expanding biological species (humans on Earth) completes its self-development into Calousians, its biggest, richest, best-possible future condition, transforming its lives and its astronomical territory accordingly.

Again, these Seven Fundamental Abilities are maximized because SciTech growth thereafter cannot increase these particular subjects further. Once you learn to travel as fast as possible through space, more SciTech cannot increase this speed further.

But new Calousian bodies and minds at the Summit are called virtually maximized. They are called maximized because their bodies and minds have fully transcended into Calousians, like human babies finally reaching age 21. But they are called virtually maximized, because, after reaching the Calousian Summit, Calousians thereafter can still grow and change, from other new knowledge, other conditions, or just because of the desire for change.

Calousians are already most distinctive, so none of these further changes they make in themselves suffice to entitle them to another name.

In sum, we have found that growing SciTech can maximize our Seven Fundamental Abilities and virtually maximize our bodies and minds, allowing us to self-transcend into Calousians. These maximizations and virtual maximizations, these limits to the benefits of SciTech growth, prove the Calousian Summit exists.

This Summit doesn't just denote an embellishment of us humans. Instead, it completes the self-transcendence of us mammal animals into a higher, far more intelligent and capable kind of beings.

What is so important here is the creation of the very new and advanced kind of beings that we will have become at the Summit. Obviously, **we have looked at our human future here primarily from our human point of view,** i.e., from what was best for us. We have assumed that if the universe has produced other ability-expanders like us elsewhere in the cosmos, those beings would also have the chance of progressing to the same Calousian Summit, just as we do.

This is the approach I took in my earlier book; *Calousia, The Best Future: Let's Get There.*

Again, the preceding chapters have proven that our long progression has a natural Calousian Summit.

But is there another way to prove the existence of this Summit?

Yes, and quite unexpectedly, it's by taking a new approach to examining how the universe actually advances.

12

THE SECOND PROOF THAT THE CALOUSIAN SUMMIT EXISTS. PART A: HOW THE ADVANCING UNIVERSE PRODUCED US

The second proof that our long progression has a natural Summit is found in the way the Advancing Universe (AU) actually progresses.

First, since we are unquestionably part of the progressing universe, let's begin this quest at the largest scale. Let's try to understand how we relatively tiny individuals, social beings, relate to the colossal universe. In other words, let's briefly review how the progressing universe produced us. This may also shed light on where our progress should take us from our own point of view.

So How Did the Universe Evolve and Produce Us?

I should state here that in order to be as objective as possible about our species and its condition, I have taken the approach of trying to see humanity as a species different from my own, one with which I have no special bond. In my mind I have sought to peer down upon humans and their activities as though from some distance away from Earth. This distance has eventually led to my seeing our species and its activities in a universal context.

As for our universe, as our knowledge of it has grown–particularly in the West–its size has expanded enormously. We once thought the universe an extremely cozy place–to us now, if not to our predecessors then. It consisted, in the West, of the lands around the Mediterranean and the canopy above with little lights in it. Eventually we learned that stars were other suns, but we still thought that our galaxy was the entire universe. Finally, just one long lifetime ago, in 1929, we began to realize that the universe was far, far bigger than we knew. At first, we thought it held many galaxies, then we thought there were some 100 billion galaxies, and now we know that the universe holds some two trillion galaxies. Our universe is a cozy place no more.

Does it nevertheless make sense to look upon our species and its activities as a natural part–conceivably even a very special part–of the colossal progressing 2 trillion galaxy universe?

Yes, I think it does. And if you don't know how the universe progresses, you can't see our relationship to it or to our true future.

Therefore, let's begin a brief review of **universal history,** that grand progression from the Big Bang to the present time. To help make it more understandable, I will, as I did with human history, cover this 13.8 billion years of history as though it, too, all took place in one year. I'll also note events of particular interest to our species.

Universal History from a Human Perspective

The universe begins with the Big Bang at the start of the first second after midnight on January 1st. A fiercely hot plasma of particles, far smaller than a golf ball, explodes violently into existence and immediately, and then repeatedly, rapidly redoubles its mass.

As the universe expands, it cools. By two o'clock in the morning, the universe has cooled enough for some atomic nuclei, mostly hydrogen and helium, to attract electrons and so to create the first atoms. These kinds of atoms are so small, so simple that on Earth they are gaseous. Since our species is about 60 percent water, some of this hydrogen in the water within us was created then.

On January 27, the first stars form, most of them being hot and fast burning giants. The "burning" in their hot cores is the consequence of hydrogen and helium nuclei fusing together into heavier nuclei. A slight loss of mass in this fusion reaction releases a vast quantity of heat energy. (Remember all that energy in the mass of the goose in Chapter 9?) This expansive heat energy in the star's interior balances the contracting gravitational energy of the star's enormous mass and so keeps the astronomical body from collapsing in upon itself. It's during this fusion activity that evolving stars synthesize many kinds of larger nuclei, including such components of our bodies as carbon, nitrogen, calcium, phosphorus, sodium, and oxygen.

When a large star's sources of energy run so low that it starts to fuse nuclei to form iron, this interaction, rather than yielding energy, absorbs it from its surroundings. The resulting lack of expansive energy pressure in the star's center means that, suddenly, the star can no longer resist its gigantic gravitational mass. The star first quickly collapses in upon itself and then explodes as a supernova, brighter than a galaxy. The extreme conditions during this explosion foster the creation of most of the larger kinds of atomic nuclei, including the iron in our blood. Large supernovas can leave behind tiny, very dense remnants–neutron stars. When these neutron stars in turn collide, the resulting intense explosions are the means the universe uses to create nuclei heavier than iron such as the silver, gold and platinum in your rings, bracelets and watches.

Supernovas and other explosions hurtle all their created atomic nuclei out into the interstellar medium where new forming stars will gravitationally draw these nuclei into themselves.

This long process produces the nuclear components of atoms and all the hundred or so stable, larger kinds of atoms that make possible rocky planets, like Earth, that would evolve around later generations of stars.

This process of stars being born, creating larger atomic nuclei, then creating white dwarfs and heavier nuclei and exploding their contents out into the interstellar medium continues through February, March, April, May, June, July, and August-and, of course, it continues today.

Note that since the atoms in our human bodies were created before the solar system formed, we have some justification for considering ourselves to be more than just earthly or solar system creatures. Of course, worms and other species can make the same claim.

However, on about September 1, in our part of our Milky Way galaxy, a cloud of dust containing hydrogen, helium, and all those heavier elements increasingly contracts until it forms the solar system, including our planet Earth.

On Earth, nearly three weeks later, around September 20, chemical evolution among the atoms and molecules eventually produces the first living creatures, single cell organisms, bacteria, that can grow, then divide into two smaller copies of themselves, and then continue growing and dividing. However, it's not until the early part of December that organisms become sophisticated enough to produce multicellular life.

On December 16, during the Cambrian period, the first simple animals evolve into existence. On December 19, vertebrates–fish–arrive on the scene. On December 22, the first large vertebrates–amphibians–begin to crawl out of the water onto the land. On the day after Christmas, December 26, the first mammals evolve–tiny tree shrew-like creatures. Dinosaurs also emerge at this time and rule until December 30.

On New Year's Eve, December 31, at about ten minutes after ten o'clock in the evening, the first beings anatomically just like us, *Homo sapiens*, appear. A little less than two minutes before midnight, the first modern humans to behave like us, with true speech, arrive. These are beings that can deliberately increase the kinds of things they can do over the generations.

Obviously, our species arrives extremely late on the universal stage, as though breathless, sweaty, and lucky to have caught the great progression at all. Whew!

Progress

Yes, this history unquestionably exhibits progress, an increasing development and complexity. But we should note that only a tiny portion of universal mass/energy actually progresses. Most of it exhibits merely change. For example, in the astronomical sphere, many stars cycle from birth to death without producing life, and in the biological sphere on Earth, while some bacteria evolved to multicellular organisms and on to us humans, other bacteria remain comparatively unchanged. In brief, only a tiny portion of cosmic mass/energy participates directly in the universal progression.

We've now briefly covered how the universe progressed and produced us humans. Is it possible to use the way the universe progresses as a second method for identifying our Calousian-creating Summit? The next chapter explores this question.

13

THE SECOND PROOF THAT THE CALOUSIAN SUMMIT EXISTS PART B: HOW THE ADVANCING UNIVERSE (AU) PROGRESSES

But is there another way to prove the existence of our greatest-future Summit? As suggested above, the answer is "yes."

Recently, in the middle of the night, instead of sleeping, I reviewed the history of the AU in my mind. I kept getting confused about some of the contents of its different stages, so the next morning, I made a summary of the process. As you will see, this summary shows the universe advancing through a series of stages in which each stage has a summit.

Does any stage reveal anything like the Calousian Summit? Let's see.

When we think of the universe, we tend to think, appropriately, of the AU's larger structures, i.e., of galaxies, galactic clusters, and super-galactic clusters, and of stars of different kinds at different stages of their different evolutions.

Furthermore, the universe as a whole and in its parts changes over time. For example, big stars change rapidly and explode, while small stars change over time very slowly and don't explode. Young galaxies, with lots of dust and blue stars, rapidly produce new stars; later, old galaxies, with almost no dust, contain red stars, and produce very few new stars. As for the entire universe, under the influence of dark energy, it keeps expanding over time.

But the primary arena where the AU doesn't just change through time but truly progresses, although this advance is often profligate and inefficient, really takes place at a smaller scale. **The AU progresses here in the sense that it creates ever larger, more complex, and more sophisticated smaller structures.** For example, it starts with energy and creates atomic particles, then it creates simple atoms, then all the rest of the larger, stable kinds of atoms, and after that simple and more complex molecules up to DNA and associated molecules. It's this advancing part of the AU that we'll focus on here.

Note that our AU does not advance through one continuous progressive process. Why? Because the universe can only advance by using the materials and the progressing formulas at hand. This means that our cosmos progresses through a sequence of stages of quite different processes. Furthermore, each stage has a summit that produces the new, advanced material for the next stage.

To accomplish this, all the AU's stages start with **two beginning-stage**-determining conditions, and all end with **two end-stage**-determining conditions.

The two beginning conditions are, first, the stage's new starting material, usually produced, as noted, by the previous stage's summit, and, second, its resulting new dominant progressing formula. The two ending conditions are its new product for the next stage–the maximizing of the starting material by its progressing formula at the summit–and then, in consequence, the progressing formula loses it utility, ending the stage.

What follows is an outline summary of these four main conditions that characterize each AU stage. To make this progression more evident, we'll omit all the universal entities and activities not directly related to the AU's progressive process.

The AU's Stage One: Creating hydrogen and helium nuclei and electrons

The new **starting material** is the Big Bang, the fiery hot universe of photons; infrared waves; no particles; inseparable matter and energy; and cosmic inflation. The dominant **progressing formula** is the nucleosynthesis of smaller nuclei.

The **new product for the next stage** at the fiery summit of Stage One is the synthesis of energy into particles, i.e., into electrons and quarks, the latter combining to form protons and neutrons, thereby completing the nuclei of hydrogen and helium atoms. The progressing **formula then loses its utility,** ending the stage. Why? It's because the expanding universe no longer has the heat or confinement to create structures larger than hydrogen and helium nuclei.

The AU's Stage Two: Creating hydrogen and helium atoms

The new **starting material** is the universe's expanding fiery hot gas of electrons, hydrogen, and helium nuclei within dark matter halos. The dominant **progressing formula** is simple atomic synthesis by cooling.

The **new product** at the summit for the next stage? The cooling allows the electromagnetic force to combine (negative) electrons with (positive) protons in hydrogen and helium nuclei, maximizing these particles into the first two kinds of atoms: hydrogen and helium atoms. The progressing **formula then loses its utility,** ending the stage. Why? Because more cooling cannot create more kinds of atoms.

The AU's Stage Three: Creating stars composed of hydrogen and helium atoms

The new **starting material** is hydrogen and helium atoms. The dominant **progressing formula** is simple stellar creation, powered by gravitation.

The **new product** at the summit for the next stage? Within halos of dark matter, gravity aggregates the new kinds of small atoms into galaxies, galactic clusters, and super-galactic clusters.

But most important, regarding the AU's advance, is that, within these large galactic structures, gravity also maximizes the hydrogen and helium atoms into simple stars at birth, that is, stars at birth composed mostly of hydrogen and helium atoms. (Why does the universe need to create stars, these huge structures, to advance? It needs the stars, as you will see, to create the rest of the needed, stable kinds of atoms.)

Why does the Stage Three progressing formula **then breaks down,** ending the stage? It's because the universe still lacks all the more complex kinds of atoms needed to create complex stars at birth.

The AU's Stage Four: Creating the rest of the stable kinds of atoms and then stars composed of all these new atoms

The new progressive **starting material** is simple stars at birth. The dominant **progressing formula** is stellar evolution, which also includes gravitation. Stellar evolution plays two essential roles here: **the first** is to synthesize all the rest of the stable, heavier kinds of elements; **the second** is to use all these additional kinds of elements to synthesize complex stars at birth.

The first **new product** at the summit for the next stage is where stellar evolution's elemental synthesis maximizes the first two kinds of atoms–hydrogen and helium–into the roughly 90 larger, stable kinds of atoms (i.e. elements) that are produced naturally. Since our focus here is on the AU's creation of ever larger small structures, we can ignore unstable atoms. These larger, heavier kinds of atoms are produced in simple stars at birth, during stellar evolution, as hydrogen, helium, and other nuclei fuse to create ever bigger nuclei with their associated electrons.

In the course of stellar evolution, the more massive stars explode, thereby creating more kinds of heavy nuclei. In addition, the neutron star remnants of some of these explosions sometimes merge explosively, creating still heavier kinds of elements. In these kind of explosions, all these roughly 90 naturally occurring kinds of stable atoms are blasted out into the interstellar medium where they are then gravitationally collected by new-forming stars.

The result is the creation of the second kind of Stage Four **new product** of stellar evolution for the next stage is complex stars at birth, i.e., stars made of all these different stable kinds of atoms. Some of these complex stars contain rocky, watery planets, the materials and habitations for the next advance.

The Stage Four progressing formula **then breaks down** in two ways. The first way it ends is because stellar evolution can't create more kinds of stable atoms than these 90 kinds. Why? Because any larger atoms would have more positive charged protons fighting each other in their nuclei, causing them to disintegrate quickly. Therefore, you can't build anything with them. The second way Stage Four ends is since no larger, long-living atoms can be created, stellar evolution cannot use them to create even more complex stars at birth.

The AU's Stage Five: Creating first life, bacteria

Stage Five's new **starting material** is complex stars at birth, particularly those with rocky, warm, watery planets (for example, Earth) containing the 90 naturally occurring kinds of stable atoms and some molecules. The dominant **progressing formula** is chemical evolution. Efficient chemical evolution requires a unique environment: stars are too hot, space is too un-confining. Earth, a rocky, watery planet circling a complex star at birth, is perfect.

The **new product** at the Stage Five summit is created as the progressing formula uses water and local heat sources (such as hydrothermal vents) and selected members of the previously created elements and molecules to develop ever larger and more complex molecules–e.g., inorganic molecules, organic molecules, sugars, amino acids, fatty acids, nucleic acids, RNA, etc. Ultimately, at the Summit, it maximizes these new chemicals into Earth's first living structures, that is, into bacteria, the largest, most complex, and most sophisticated structures that the advancing universe has so far created locally.

The progressing **formula then breaks down,** because Stage Five's chemical evolution formula thereafter loses its species-creating dominance to a new formula: biological evolution. This is because the biological evolution process can create more kinds of species faster and more efficiently than chemical evolution can.

The AU's Stage Six: Creating us human ability expanders

Stage Six's new **starting materials** are bacteria (and possibly archaea). The dominant **progressing formula,** in consequence, is biological evolution, specifically, species synthesis, i.e., the creation of ever more complex kinds of organisms. Here, favorable mutations give the resulting new organisms a greater chance for reproductive success in their environments. The consequence over time is new bodily processes, new structures, and new species. Unfavorable mutations result in diminished reproductive success, and often lead to extinction.

The **new products** at the Stage Six summit are new organic molecules, millions of different kinds of species, and ecosystems. But the most crucial new summit product of Stage Six for the next stage, regarding the AU, is the maximizing of this biological progression by the creation of us humans.

Why are we humans the Summit species? Again, it's not because of the usual static characterizations we give ourselves, such as being wise, tool users, and culture bearers. Instead, it's because we are the first species on Earth capable of expanding our abilities over the generations through knowledge growth. We are Earth's first self-improving, potentially self-transforming and therefore self-transcending species.

The progressing **formula then breaks down,** ending the Stage Six. This breakdown occurs because the biological evolution formula of mutations and selections loses its dominance. This in turn happens because if the AU is to continue its long advance hereafter, the best strategy for creating new and more advanced biological species is not biological evolution. This system is too uncertain in producing species, let alone in producing new and more advanced species. The best strategy henceforth will be to allow humans to improve themselves with the new progressing formula of SciTech growth and adjustments. This capacity makes us humans the new material at hand that the AU needs in Stage Six to continue its progression.

Our species' self-expanding characteristic will become more evident when we purposefully manipulate our DNA, as we are now learning to do. This new ability will allow us to perform this self-improving function of ourselves far faster and better than the old formula of biological evolution.

How the AU Determines the Stage Seven Summit

One great advantage of these four stage-determining conditions is that this approach **can reveal the AU's Stage-**

Seven Summit, the Summit of the stage that we humans participate in. This is because once you know the first two of our Stage Seven's four conditions, you will have substantial clues about the last two conditions. Furthermore, because this approach depends upon how the universe actually progresses, it provides a scientific way of identifying our Stage Seven Summit.

So, let's see what the AU's four Summit-identifying conditions reveal about our Stage Seven Summit.

The AU's Stage Seven: Creating Calousians

Stage Seven's new **starting material** is our human species. Why do we have this honor? Again, it's because our intelligence, curiosity, and social and manipulative skills make us the first and only species on our planet able to keep improving itself over the generations through knowledge growth.

What is our **progressing formula?** As noted, it's expanding our human condition through knowledge growth and adjustments. Particularly, it's through (A) SciTech growth, leading to increasing abilities, (B) accumulating this knowledge socially and then adjustments to the resulting changing conditions, and (A') then creating new SciTech growth. This approach is a faster and more purposeful growth method for the AU than biological evolution.

So, what parts of us should our growing SciTech keep improving to advance the AU?

It's the three parts of us. These are: first, our fundamental abilities; second, our bodies and minds; and, third, how we live.

(Yes, we are finally beginning to consider this promised third part of us.)

So far in our Summit proof, what's best for our species has also been the best way for the AU to continue its progression. But how do these first two AU Stage Seven stage-determining conditions reveal our Stage Seven's Summit? In other words, what is the Advancing Universe's new Stage Seven product at the Summit?

The new product for the next stage is the maximized and virtually maximized three parts of us. Why?

Remember, in Stage 2, nuclei and electrons were maximized into atoms, and, in Stage 3, the simple atoms were maximized into simple stars, and, in Stage 4, the two kinds of atoms were maximized into the 90 kinds of stable atoms, and, in Stage 5, these atoms and a few kinds of molecules were maximized into bacteria, and, in Stage 6, bacteria were maximized into us humans.

It makes consistent sense, therefore, that, in Stage 7, we biologically created *Homo sapiens sapiens*, mammal animals, must maximize ourselves into a higher kind of entity. In our case this means that we must maximize ourselves, i.e., the three parts of us, into the higher universal kind of beings called Calousians.

And here are six additional reasons why, to complete our AU's Stage 7, we must maximize the three parts of us.

First, because these areas are so distinctive and so important to our species fulfilling its potential. **Second,**

there's no logical place short of this maximizing to stop. **Third**, maximizing would give us the greatest advantage. **Fourth**, those acquiring all the tools, techniques, and knowledge to expand these parts of us as much as possible could probably soon perform almost any other possible manipulations of us. **Fifth**, this is what all beings like us in the universe are probably doing for the same reasons. And **Sixth**, maximizing ourselves takes us to the AU's Stage-Seven Summit. It therefore completes the AU's Stage Seven and, of course, it also fulfills our species' astonishing potential.

How do we do this maximizing?

We will need to discover these answers for ourselves. Regarding the **Seven Fundamental Abilities** most important to our species completing the AU's Stage Seven, we will need to keep growing SciTech until we maximize these abilities, as I showed in Chapter 9. To repeat, these seven abilities are: (1) biological, (2) elemental, and (3) astronomical, the three components of our environment; (4) communication and (5) transportation; and (6) access to energy and (7) power devices, i.e., engines and motors.

Regarding how we maximize our **bodies and minds**, another requirement for a successful AU Stage Seven, we will need to virtually maximize them as we saw in Chapter 10.

Note that we've already made great progress, since our hunt-and-gather days, in both our fundamental abilities and how we live. But we've made no advance whatsoever in physically changing our bodies and minds. And we humans are the key third part in our Stage Seven's advance. So if we don't advance our bodies and minds, our Stage Seven here cannot make its usual advances here, either.

So to complete the AU's 7th Stage here, we must make great changes in ourselves. We must virtually maximize our bodies and minds until we self-transcend into our Stage Seven's universal Calousian Summit beings. Fortunately, we are now just beginning to acquire this essential knowledge for maximizing ourselves.

What about maximizing this **how-we-live category?** Like the other two parts of us, how we live changes as SciTech grows, i.e., the more we grow our knowledge and abilities, the more we change how we live. So in our future, the more we expand our abilities and improve ourselves, the more we can expect us humans to continue changing how we live.

What subjects are included in this "how we live" category?

They include: social (family, friends, societies, governance); SciTech (the level attained, education); environment (natural and man-made, where we live on Earth and elsewhere, housing); economy (agricultural, small-scale urban, working at home, small businesses, corporate factories with large scale production, high tech state of advancement); transportation (means, costs); communication (speech, writing, phones, computers, radio, TV); access to energy (cost, availability); food (preparation, waste); clothing (head to toe; regarding weather, activities); the arts (painting, sculpture, music, dance, etc.), and, of course, our knowledge (growing, saving, distribution ability, etc.)

How do we maximize this third part of us at the Summit?

As noted, this maximization will primarily be the reasonable response to the advancement of the other two parts of us; namely, our Seven Fundamental Abilities and our human bodies and minds and, of course, to our governing environment.

So, again, how do we maximize this third part of us? In truth, we don't now know. In consequence, we just must keep experimenting in this area as our SciTech grows, our bodies and minds change, and our abilities increase.

But we can make a significant assumption about maximizing this third part of us now: it is that those who are wise enough to maximize the first two parts of us (the

Seven Fundamental Abilities and our bodies and minds) must also be clever enough to maximize how Summit Beings live in their particular environments. In other words, we can expect that at the Summit these beings will give themselves the best possible economy, society, governance, culture, environments, etc.

Note that Summit Beings may well change how they live after reaching the Summit, just as they will change their bodies-and-minds part. Therefore, how Summit Beings live when expanded to the limit, must also be considered a virtual maximization.

What then happens after we succeed in maximizing all the parts of ourselves?

Of course, the Stage Seven **progressing formula breaks down,** ending the stage, just as it did in all the previous AU stages. Our Stage Seven progression ends because growing SciTech, having maximized the Seven Fundamental Abilities and virtually maximized our bodies and minds and how we live, loses its ability to expand these parts of us further. These advances will have become virtually as great as they can be. Or, to put this another way, our SciTech, tools, and knowledge at the Summit are so great that any changes Calousians might later want to make in the three parts of us could also have been made soon upon first reaching the Summit.

Again, this maximizing and virtual maximizing of the three parts of us may at first sound unrealistic and extreme, and it's certainly far from our present experience. Yes, seeing this future reality requires us to think much bigger than before. But think of this Summit future as our hunt-

and-gather ancestors of 20,000 years ago might consider our lives today. They would judge descriptions of our present way of life as far too extreme to be believable. They wouldn't even have words for such things as walls, doors, windows, and basements, not to mention stores, banks, iPhones, and rocket ships. So please try hard to understand the extraordinarily different future that's possible ahead.

This story of how the Advancing Universe produced us humans contains much detail. To clarify, I am enclosing the following chart:

A Chart of the Advancing Universe

Note: Most of the universe just changes, but a relatively small part–the Advancing Universe–actually progresses. This Advancing Universe must always work with the material at hand. Therefore it cannot progress in one long process; instead, it must advance through a series of very different stages and processes, as follows.

STAGE 1

Synthesizing simple nuclei and electrons

New material: Big Bang, intense storm of sub-atomic particles, quarks, etc.

New progressing formula: nucleosynthesis of smallest nuclei.

New material at Stage Summit: hydrogen and helium nuclei plus electrons.

Progressing formula then loses its utility: the expanding universe no longer provides both the heat and confinement to create larger nuclei.

STAGE 2
Synthesizing simple atoms

New material (from previous Stage): hydrogen and helium nuclei and electrons.

The resulting new progressing formula: simple atomic synthesis by cooling, electromagnetism.

New material at Stage Summit: hydrogen and helium atoms.

Progressing formula then loses its utility: more cooling cannot create larger atoms.

STAGE 3
Synthesizing simple stars at birth

New material (from previous Stage): hydrogen and helium atoms.

The resulting new progressing formula: simple stellar synthesis by gravity.

New material at Stage Summit: simple stars at birth composed of hydrogen and helium atoms.

Progressing formula then loses its utility: more gravity cannot create more complex stars at birth.

STAGE 4

(a) Synthesizing the rest of the stable atoms
(b) Synthesizing complex stars at birth with rocky, watery planets

New material (from previous Stage): stars at birth composed of hydrogen and helium atoms.

The resulting new progressing formula: stellar evolution and gravitation.

New material at Stage Summit: (a) all stable atoms now synthesized; (b) rocky planets with water synthesized.

Progressing formula then loses its utility: (a) because any larger atoms produced would be unstable; (b) these unstable atoms would therefore be incapable of creating more complex stars and planets.

STAGE 5
Synthesizing first life

New material (from previous Stage): on a rocky, watery planet, all stable atoms and some small molecules.

The resulting new progressing formula: chemical evolution.

New material at Stage Summit: creation of first life: bacteria, possibly archaea.

Progressing formula then loses its utility: chemical evolution loses dominance for creating new kinds of organisms to biological evolution.

STAGE 6
Synthesizing Homo sapiens

New material (from previous Stage): bacteria, archaea.

The resulting new progressing formula: biological evolution.

New material at Stage Summit: Homo sapiens, sapiens.

Progressing formula then loses its utility: biological evolution loses its dominance to the growth of knowledge and abilities.

STAGE 7

Synthesizing Calousians

New material (from previous Stage): Homo sapiens, sapiens.

The resulting new progressing formula: growth of knowledge and abilities.

New material at Stage Summit: Calousians.

Progressing formula then loses its utility: expect knowledge and abilities growth to lose its dominance to another progressive process.

STAGE 8

?

New material (from previous Stage): Calousians.

The resulting new progressing formula: ?

New material at Stage Summit: ?

Progressing formula then loses its utility: ?

Do Calousians know everything?

Of course not. We should think of Calousians as those who have fulfilled their species' self-developing potential at the Summit. Yes, Calousians can never travel faster or find new energy sources, but they can learn and grow in other ways, just as mature humans can.

In sum, it's evident now that the universe has progressed primarily on the small scale. It has advanced from energy to particles, to simple atoms, to complex atoms, to ever more complex inorganic and organic molecules, to bacteria, to complex single celled organisms, to ever larger and more complex multicellular organisms, to our self-advancing species, and eventually, if all goes well, will progress to Calousians and Calousias.

Does the universe employ this same stepwise advance elsewhere in the universe as it has on Earth? Being aware of only one example, we don't yet know. But wouldn't the universe elsewhere still need to create particles before atoms? And complex molecules before creating life? And human-like creatures before creating highly advanced Summit Beings? Yes, it would seem that elsewhere, too, the Advancing Universe would always need to advance with the materials on hand in stages.

Does the Advancing Universe have a Stage Eight? It looks probable, but we just don't yet know.

Summary

So, where should our human progress take us? You have seen, both from a human-centered point of view and from the way the AU actually progresses, that the answer is the same: **to our progression's Summit**. In other words, all of us humans participate in one and the same universal Great Progression. And since this Calousian Summit is our biggest, richest, best-possible future, this truth gives all of us humans, for the first time, the same astonishing new purpose: namely, to strive to reach this greatest-future Summit. We should do this for ourselves, for our families, for our species–to enjoy ever better lives–and for the AU, too, because our self-transcendence into Calousians is the only way the AU can complete its Stage Seven here.

Are there any other proofs that the Calousian Summit exists? We'll explore this interesting question in the next chapter.

14

THE THIRD PROOF THAT THE CALOUSIAN SUMMIT EXISTS

Since SciTech growth is the primary engine of our Great Progression, and since SciTech is capable of endless growth, how can there be a Summit to our Great Progression? Shouldn't we progress endlessly? No. And here is the third proof of the Summit's existence. But before we present it, let's quickly review the first two proofs.

Proof #1: Because Growing SciTech Reaches Natural Maximums or Virtual Maximums to How Much It Can Keep Improving the Three Parts of Our Species.

The first proof of Calousia's existence comes from my first book. This approach found the Summit primarily from our species' point of view–asking what condition would give our species the biggest, richest, best-possible future.

The answer was to maximize or virtually maximize the maximizable areas crucial to our species' self-development. These areas include both the Seven Fundamental Abilities noted above plus the transcendence of our human bodies and minds into the higher Summit beings called Calousians.

The impressive size of these categories when maximized; the enormous accumulation of knowledge, tools, and techniques; their great importance to us in our self-development; and the fact that our Seven Fundamental Abilities, once maximized, cannot thereafter be increased and that virtually any increase in the other two parts of us–our bodies and minds and how we live–could soon be accomplished upon becoming Calousian: all of this makes the Calousian Summit distinctive. It divides all true advanced knowledge-expanders into two great groups, the Calousians and those less advanced than Calousians. Calousians, of course, will vary in their abilities, as humans do, but all are considered part of the same great, high category.

Proof #2: Because Reaching the Calousian Summit is the Natural, Logical Way an AU's Stage Seven Ends

You have seen that the AU needs to advance by stages because it can only advance with the materials at hand and by the progressing formula that the new materials make possible. So each stage advances with the same two beginning rules and the same two ending rules.

When we got to the AU's Stage Seven, our human part of the AU, we found that we were the new material: we were the first earthly species that could keep improving itself over the generations through knowledge growth. Our progressing formula was essentially (A) SciTech growth, (B) the social accumulation of this knowledge and adjustments thereto, and then (A') new SciTech growth.

Knowing these two beginning rules for how the AU's Stage Seven advances, we have been able to predict the results of the last two rules.

Can the AU make such predictions? No. It has no brain. It just proceeds as best it can. In contrast, we in Stage Seven are the first components in the AU's long advance to be aware of what we and the AU are doing. And, unlike earlier AU advances, we need to know where to go, or else we wouldn't do the essential organizing to get there.

What did the predictions tell us? We found that the AU advanced here best if we maximized the three parts of us.

And what is the second end-stage rule? It is that Stage Seven ends.

Why? Because that's the Summit; growing SciTech thereafter cannot increase the maximized entities or much increase the virtually maximized entities.

In other words, whether we look at our future from the point of view of what's best for us humans, or from the way the AU actually advances, the consequence is the same. The goal is for us to reach the Calousian Summit.

But is there a third way to foresee why the Calousian greatest-future Summit exists? Yes.

Proof #3: The Sculptor's Mold Shows How the Summit of Calousian-Creation Is the Natural Consequence of Growth Meeting Limits

This approach is just another way of looking at the AU's Stage Seven Calousian-Creation process and its natural ending, of seeing it all as a single unified process.

Those who explore humanity's future concentrate on the expanding abilities part of our long progressing process.

They try to foresee where growing SciTech will expand our abilities and ourselves into specific futures, perhaps 50 or 200 years away, and how this will change the way we live. These are worthy endeavors, but they deal with only the first half of our longterm, progressive, abilities-expanding evolution.

Let's now explore this **other half of our progressive evolution,** the part that has been little considered until now, i.e., the great group of universal limits to the benefits of ever-growing SciTech. I call this other half of the Great Progression the **Calousian-Creating Mold**.

Consider the sculptor's mold. The sculptor, wanting to create a statue of a human figure, for example like **Rodin** creating *The Thinker*, creates a mold, the interior of which is, of course, shaped to produce the desired statue. The sculptor then pours the glowing molten metal, in this case bronze, into the mold until it's filled. When the metal cools, the mold is removed to reveal the finished sculpture of *The Thinker.*

Our Stage Seven abilities-expanding evolution may be thought of as taking place within a kind of universal sculptor's mold. This mold itself consists of all the universe's limits to the growth of the three parts of us. If we keep growing SciTech until we maximize or virtually maximize these three parts of us, this is analogous to pouring molten metal until the mold is filled.

Where the sculptor's mold transformed metal into a statue of a human, the Calousian-Creating Mold transforms us humans–or Ability-Expanders, if we would see ourselves as an example of a universal type–into Calousians. This transformation would complete the AU's Stage Seven and perhaps commence its Stage Eight.

In other words, we can think of our species' entire, long, abilities-expanding evolution as a system consisting of an expanding force eventually meeting an immovable object. The expanding force, arising from our species' unique character, is that we can keep increasing our abilities, improving our bodies, and improving how we live over the generations through knowledge growth, most particularly through SciTech growth. The immovable object is the universal mold, that great cluster of universal limits to the benefits of continuing SciTech growth among the three parts of us.

The universal laws and conditions, evident locally, ultimately determine which abilities our growing SciTech can give us and which it cannot. In consequence, we can say that we humans do the growing and the universe–i.e., universal conditions–determines the results.

This expanding-force/immovable-object interaction proves the existence of a Calousian greatest-future Summit to our long progression.

Why? Because at the Summit, the expanding force aspect, which has been active throughout our long progressive evolution, maximizes. It meets the immovable object. In consequence, the process, the interaction, breaks down. Regarding the limited aspects of our Seven Fundament Abilities, SciTech can grow them no more. Regarding the other two parts of us (our minds and bodies and how Calousians live), they are virtually maximized. This means that at the Summit we already have enough SciTech, tools, techniques, and knowledge now to make any possible changes in these other two parts of us that we might in the future want to make.

These are the limits we sought to SciTech's limitless growth. We will have reached our state of mature self-development. This completion of our expanding force/immovable-object interaction is the proof that the Summit exists.

It's just like the AU's Stage Two reaching its summit when small atomic synthesis and cooling can no longer create new atoms, or when its Stage Four, stellar evolution, reaches its summit because it can create no more stable atoms after those first 90. The resulting maximized abilities, the changes they make in us, and their economic and social consequences, are what give Calousia its distinctive character as our biggest, richest, best-possible future.

Summary

This chapter proves the existence of a natural greatest-future Summit to our part of the AU's Stage Seven's long progression **in three ways.** The **first** way was essentially from our species' growth point of view, i.e., the changes that would give us the biggest, richest, best-possible future. The **second** was in how the AU naturally progresses. And the **third** was the Calousian-Creating Mold, that is, by seeing our long progression whole, as an expanding-force, immovable-object interaction.

You are now aware that the Calousian Summit exists. You know that our species' long, self-expanding progression, our species' biggest achievement so far, can naturally progress to a superb, self-transforming summit. This new knowledge is what gives our species the new astonishing purpose of reaching this biggest, richest, best possible future.

And what is this astonishing purpose? It's for our species to self-transcend into the higher kind of beings called Calousians. I say more of this in Chapter 21. This completes this book's Part I.

Nevertheless, there is really much more that you should know about this new, potential summit future of our species. For example, what is this Calousian Summit like? How far away is it? Does the AU have a Stage Eight? And why is the existence of the Calousian Summit revolutionary in so many ways, like changing our view of races and nations, and even our understanding of what we humans are? These are some of the questions we'll answer in Part II.

But what's the great advantage of learning that the Calousian Summit exists? The next chapter, the first in Part II, will explain that, too.

Part II

ABOUT THE CALOUSIAN GREATEST-FUTURE SUMMIT

15

WHY IS IDENTIFYING THE CALOUSIAN SUMMIT ADVANTAGEOUS TO US?

This next book section is "About the… Summit." Since "Summit" here has a number of quite different meanings, the following Chart should help clarify them.

Aspects Of the Summit

1. The Summit completes our species' Great Progression, that enormous growth of human knowledge and abilities since our hunt-and-gather days.

2. The Summit's name is "Calousia," (Kah-lou'-see-ah) classical Greek for "beautiful existence," not because it's utopian, but because it gives humanity its biggest, richest, best-possible future.

3. The Summit is where we humans complete our self-development by transcending into higher universal Calousian beings. We do this by maximizing the seven

fundamental abilities, and virtually maximizing our human mind and bodies and how we live.

4. The Summit is when we humans complete the AU's Stage Seven locally, and it might possibly mark the highest level of the AU's progression.

5. And, finally, the Summit is when our Calousian descendants, potential AU managers, probably commence their AU's Stage Eight locally.

So, again, why is identifying the Calousian Summit so advantageous?

First, remember that our long progression from hunters-and-gatherers to the way most people in the advanced part of the world live today is our species' greatest achievement. And this progression continues. It's the undertaking that most characterizes us humans. Therefore, knowing where our progression should take us is also of extraordinary importance.

Second, let's note the very important disadvantages of our remaining unaware of the Calousian Summit. In unawareness, we might at any time during our long, Great Progression think that we have advanced as much as we can.

We might then decide to focus on short term goals. With no particular goal to aim for, we would lack the incentive to manage our accelerating process in order to succeed in it. We'd just continue racing blindly down the dangerous, short term, increasingly chaotic path to our eventual extinction. So discontinuing the dangerous activities caused by our old ignorance is the second great advantage to identifying the Summit.

The third advantage of identifying the Calousian Summit is that it makes us aware, for the first time in our human history, of the whole Calousian Creation Process–the advance of our species from technological novices to maximizing masters. With awareness, we better understand the scope of the process, how it works, why it makes sense, where we are in the process, and why we are there.

The fourth advantage of foreseeing aspects of the Summit is that we perceive, for the first time, how vastly superior this maximized future–this fully realized, mature state of our self-development–is to our present situation.

The fifth advantage, now that we are aware of the superiority of the Summit, is that it offers us–again for the first time in human history–a new goal, a primary purpose: it's to deliberately strive to reach this Calousian Summit.

Until now, our species has been like a man who can't get home because he doesn't know he has one, and so has no reason to try. We haven't known that our Calousian Creation offers us a "home," an advantageous Summit, so we have had no reason to attempt to reach it. But now that we know Calousia exists and that it fulfills our species' extraordinary potential, it makes sense to strive aggressively for this Calousian goal. This identifies the astonishing purpose that our species' has long needed. I'll say more about our primary purpose in Chapter 21.

The sixth advantage of identifying the Calousian Summit is that we become aware of the character of the Summit and where, in future time, the Summit might be. We can therefore more effectively manage our way toward it. We can see better where we are now in our progressive process and how far away we are from the Summit. And because we know how Calousian Creation works, we are better positioned to choose and then take the difficult, necessary steps required to reach this Calousian Summit. For example, we know better what SciTech we must acquire. We also have a better chance of managing the accelerating introduction of new technologies and their consequences (economic, social, and environmental).

Finally, we can begin to think productively about what fulfilling the potential of our species means, about what we might want to be at the Summit, and about how we want to live there. I'll say more about management in this book's Part III.

This is why identifying Calousia's existence is so advantageous.

But why should this new perception be revolutionary? The next chapter explains.

16

REVOLUTION #1: THE REVOLUTIONARY CHANGES IN PERCEPTION THAT COME FROM IDENTIFYING THE CALOUSIAN SUMMIT

In the last chapter, we noted the advantages of identifying the Calousian Summit.Now, let's see why our perception of the Calousian Summit revolutionary. This revolutionary point is so important that it's worth focusing on in its own chapter here.

This chapter is the first of seven new, revolutionary changes in either perception or in major socio-economic conditions that will help us better understand our changing conditions and therefore will also help us succeed in reaching our long Great Progression's Summit.

First, let's look at our perceptions before this first revolutionary change.

As noted, for most of our species' existence we hardly advanced at all, so we had no progress to become aware of. But over the last few thousand years, and especially in more recent times –e.g., during the Industrial Revolution– yes, we finally realized that we were advancing, and at an accelerating rate, too.

But today we still have no idea of where our progress should take us. We remain a lost species. We are like caterpillars unaware of their butterfly future.

And being lost, as previously noted, it's understandable that we moved in many wrong and dangerous directions that make our advance to Calousia increasingly difficult. These missteps include: allowing our population to surge, our environment to degrade, our world governance to remain fragmented, and our nuclear and biological weapons to grow, for the first time ever, great enough to exterminate us all.

Now let's look at the details of this first revolutionary change.

1. For the first time, we see the enormous mountain ahead of us and recognize its Summit. Our view is not yet clear. It's hazy. (For example, we still do not know how fast we can travel, or all the changes we will make in our bodies.) But at last, after passing through many long valleys and over the tops of many hills that we incorrectly thought were the Summit, we now finally see that high true Summit ahead of us. It's an unexpected surprise. Is that, we wonder, really where our long trail ends? **Do we really need to travel *that* far and *that* high?** The answer is "Yes." We now perceive that reaching this Summit is a revolutionary greater task than almost any of us have heretofore imagined.

2. We also perceive that the Summit promises revolutionary greater benefits than we have heretofore imagined. We see at once that this new Summit world, with its maximized abilities, bodies, and how we live, is vastly superior to our present condition, and that as we advance we will enjoy ever bigger, richer, and better lives. This evidence of the much better world ahead encourages us to wonder, for the first time, if it makes practical sense to deliberately try for this new Summit ahead.

3. This identification of the Summit doesn't just greatly change our perception of our bodies and minds; it changes our perception of **what we humans really are.**

We become aware that we are not primarily the static beings we always thought we were. Specifically, we are not just wise, tool users, and culture bearers, and we are not restricted to our present form, like all other Earth-life is, to the process of mutations and selection.

Instead, Summit knowledge awakens us to the perception that we humans are inherently and uniquely a dynamic self-developing and self-transforming species. At last we realize what we really are, and it's a revolutionary change compared to our earlier static view of ourselves. We'll consider this point further in Chapter 20.

4. Knowledge of our Summit future also revolutionarily changes our perception of **our whole progression.** It makes sense of it. It helps us understand our increasingly fast-changing world. It puts into place the hunt-and-gather world that we came from. It tells us, for the first time, where we are in our progression, why we are where we are, and how much further we must advance to reach our

progression's natural Summit. Heretofore, we tended to think that we were about as advanced as we practically could be while facing a cloudy, uncertain future; now we much better appreciate the considerable distance still to go. And we more deeply realize that we participate in a Great, Self-Developing Progression.

In addition, knowledge of the Summit **helps reveal how our Calousian-Creation Progression works, and it emphasizes the major role that growing SciTech knowledge plays in advancing us.** Now we perceive not only where we should go, but much of what we must do to get there. For example, we know that if we can keep our SciTech growing, and keep adjusting and advancing in our Calousian-Creation Progression, we will reach the Calousian Summit. We know that we must keep advancing our fundamental abilities, and therefore how we live, and we know that in the future we will increasingly transform our bodies and minds as we transcend into the higher future universal beings called Calousians. With this revolutionary change in perception, our fast-changing world of SciTech growth no longer mystifies us.

5. All of these new perceptions bring about a revolutionary change in **human purpose**. Heretofore, our fragmented species had no single purpose, except, perhaps, to survive. Individuals thought first of their families. They gave their allegiance to their nations and followed their religions.

But now, with this new perception of the extraordinary Summit ahead, for the first time in human existence, we expect that more and more members of our species will adopt the one, very new, and most important goal, that is, to reach this brilliant, new, Calousian future, and to reach it as soon as possible. We understand that this goal is best for our human species and, as noted in Chapter 13, best for the progressing universe as well.

Why should this Summit be our goal?

Again, we perceive that it's our species' knowledge-growing character that gives us the unique opportunity to keep improving ourselves. And we see that it's advantageous to keep making these improvements as long as possible, that is, until we finally grow as far as we possibly can by maximizing or virtually maximizing our three parts: our abilities, our bodies and minds, and how we live.

Note again that we perceive this Calousian-Creation Summit goal as not just for some humans. It's for all humans.

Why for all humans?

Again, it's because this ability to advance ourselves is the most unique and important characteristic of our species, and because we are all restricted to limited lives when we don't advance, and because we all benefit with expanded lives when we do advance.

Note, again, that almost everything we individual humans do, on balance, either helps or harms our Calousian advance. As for helping the advance, reading this book has probably already revealed some pro-Calousian steps that you can take or have taken; others are suggested in Chapter 33.

As for **harming** our advance, when the numbers of our human population are very high, as they are now, almost everything we do–what we eat and drink what we buy and sell, our businesses, our entertainments, how we live, the children we have, etc.–harms our advance by consuming energy and resources and thereby diminishing our environment's ability to continue supporting our advance. Of course, our recycling, our use of appropriate energy, etc., helps reduce this harm.

But, as Chapter 22 will make clear, many cultures around the world today have not yet realized that all of us humans participate in the same, great Calousian-Creating Progression. Many of these groups, being originally long isolated from the rest of the world, were less advanced in the Great Progression which was not their fault. And many of these isolated groups, have tended to essentially remain in their same hunt-and-gather or early farming worlds.

These isolated groups should cease remaining backward in our one Great Progression. It hurts them, leaving them at a less advanced level, and it hurts the rest of us, because our modern world is far from perfect, and we need them to join us moderns and play their rightful, meaningful role in helping all our species as we advance to our progression's natural, superior Summit.

6. All of these new perceptions allow us, for the first time in human existence, to begin to **rationally plan** an approach to our newly revealed Summit that can be successful. This is a revolutionary change in our view of how to approach our future. It's now apparent that we can't reach Calousia with our present disorganized approach. The task before us is just too large, complex, dynamic, and

fast changing. Therefore, to succeed in this last part of Calousian Creation, as with all very large tasks, we perceive for the first time that, to be successful, we must take charge of our own Great Progression. There's nobody else to do it. **We must create a new, world-wide management appropriate for the huge new task we face.** In Chapter 30, this book will identify the **seven new organizations** essential to our success. This Calousian-Creation management, too, is a revolutionary change in perception from our past views.

In sum, these **six new perceptions** are unquestionably revolutionary. They complete the **first revolution** that is **essential** if our species is to be successful. It's the perception, for the first time in human existence, by our lost species wandering in dangerous directions, that our long progression must have a natural, vastly superior Summit.

You now understand that humanity has the primary purpose of reaching the Calousian Summit. But why is this Calousian future our species' biggest, richest, best-possible existence? The next chapter explains.

17

WHY IS CALOUSIA OUR BIGGEST, RICHEST, BEST-POSSIBLE FUTURE?

Calousia is the mature Summit State of Calousian Creation. It's like a human growing to age 21. Just as mature humans can keep growing in abilities after age 21–fortunately–so can Calousians. So when we've considered comparatives like "biggest, richest," etc., our reference has been from where humanity is now compared to the Calousian Summit. We expect that more advanced Calousian systems, like older humans, will acquire more abilities.

So with this concept in mind, let's discuss why Calousia is our species' biggest, richest, best-possible future.

It's our **biggest future** because our seven fundamental abilities will have risen from near zero to become maximized and the other two parts of us will also have risen from very low to become virtually maximized. In other words, those three parts of us, our seven fundamental abilities, our bodies and minds, and how we live, which are most important to both us and to Calousians, will have become as big as universal conditions allow. Calousia is the biggest also for all the other maximums we would naturally acquire in areas beyond these three specific parts of us. All these areas are the biggest–the maximum–because growing SciTech cannot increase them further.

Calousia is our **richest future** partially because of all the experiences and advantages possible as a consequence of maximizing, or virtually maximizing, the great breadth and depth of the three parts of ourselves and all the other knowledge and abilities acquired during the course of reaching the Summit. Perhaps the most important reason Calousia is our richest future is because humans have become Calousians, those individuals with maximized minds, senses, and bodies, and with all their acquired knowledge, tools, and techniques. Compare a hunter-gatherer's charcoal drawing to a present day person streaming a movie on an iPad or looking down from an airplane window at the passing worlds below. And then imagine all the further advantages acquired by Calousians–the experiences, the choices, the incomparable richness unknown to the less-developed Pre-Calousians.

Finally, Calousia is our **best-possible future** because having maximized our Seven Fundamental Abilities and virtually maximized our bodies and minds, it's reasonable to assume that those smart enough to acquire all those abilities should also be wise enough to achieve the best possible way to live. Among other things, this means providing Calousians with the best economic, social, political, environmental, and cultural benefits.

This maximizing or virtually maximizing of the three parts of ourselves is why Calousia is our species' biggest, richest, best-possible future. And, again, this declaration comes from a human, Pre-Calousian point of view. Calousians, being higher, superior kinds of beings, should have other, greater best-possible futures.

Why is the Summit "Humanity's Greatest Future?"
If the growth of human knowledge since our hunt-and-gather days is humanity's greatest achievement; and if we reach our Great Progression's Summit by maximizing or virtually maximizing the crucial aspects of the three parts of us and therefore transcend into new Calousians; and if these activities create our biggest, richest, best-possible future; then it's evident that the Calousian Summit is "Humanity's Greatest Future."

In the next chapter, we'll consider not only why Calousia is distinctive, but why it may be far, far more than that.

18

WHY IS CALOUSIA A DISTINCTIVE, UNIVERSAL SUMMIT?

I've explained that Calousia is the distinctive Summit to our species' single, great, abilities-expanding progression.

Now let's consider the **distinctiveness of Calousia from a universal perspective.** Assuming that Calousia is a possibility for us here on Earth, it's probable that the universe has created or will create, either in our galaxy or in the two trillion other galaxies, many Calousias. If so, all the Calousias would have command of essentially the same maximized communication and transportation abilities, and so all would be similar in the size of the sphere of the universe that they could directly influence in reasonable time. All would have access to the same range of inanimate sources of power, like engines and motors. All would know how to access the largest stores of cheap energy. And these similar powers would occur throughout the three parts of these beings.

As a consequence, if we could examine many groups of abilities-expanders around the universe, assuming they exist, we could readily distinguish the Calousians from all those who are less advanced. In other words, Calousia is distinctive. These beings would be obviously superior to all those of lesser ability.

Why Is Calousia the Summit of Calousian Creation?

What if some Calousias are more advanced than others? For example, it's reasonable, isn't it, to expect that older, longer-existing Calousias will have grown more knowledgeable and capable than younger or new Calousias and so exert a wider and deeper influence over their astronomical territory? And since SciTech knowledge can still grow after humans have reached Calousia, how can Calousia be the Summit of Calousian Creation?

The answer is that all Calousias can boast of the same, enormous, basic capacity, since all are based on having maximized or virtually maximized the three parts of themselves. And this capacity, remember, in just part of the realm of synthesis, allows them to create any possible chemicals from atoms and any possible living creatures from on-the-shelf chemicals.

In other words, since all Calousias enjoy the same extraordinary and basic technical ability, the differences between the more and less advanced Calousias are not sufficient to consider some Calousias as being of a different order than the others. In consequence, then, we can consider all Calousias to be essentially equal.

In this sense, Calousians are like humans, who may be young or old, large or small, brilliant or dull, yet we recognize all to be of the same species and distinctly more advanced than chimpanzees, dolphins, and great apes.

So far, we've noted that one can readily distinguish Calousias from those less advanced in Calousian Creation and clearly equated with other Calousias. Is it possible, then, to consider Calousia to be more than a distinctive future and more than the Summit of Calousian Creation?

Let's consider this larger possibility now.

Why May Calousias Be the Summit State of the Progressive Evolution of the Universe?

Heretofore in this book, you have had to think bigger. Now you must think far bigger still. (Authors have such amazing powers over readers.) You must consider no less than the significance of Calousias in relation to the progressive development of the entire universe.

As previously noted, after the Big Bang, universal mass-energy elaborated itself into galaxies, stars, and planets, the theater for the next act. Then, under favorable conditions, such as those on our planet, atoms and molecules aggregated to create life. The biological evolution this initiated progressed until it produced us abilities-expanders, human beings who can participate in Calousian Creation. All along, we have been playing our appropriate technology-expanding part in Calousian Creation and have been working our way ever faster toward Calousia.

At Calousia, evolving, progressing mass energy will have created two of its highest creations at their most advanced state, namely, the Calousian individual and Calousia itself. (As noted in Chapter 11, Calousia is a system, consisting of Calousian individuals, their society, their territory, and all the material entities associated with them.)

If there is one state in the knowledge-expanding, Calousian-creating progressive aspect of universal evolution that is so distinctive, knowledge-filled, and capable as to constitute **the Summit of the progressive evolution of the universe, Calousia seems to be that condition**.

We have noted that Calousia is not only the Summit of the AU's Stage Seven, but the start of the AU's Stage Eight. We will consider Stage Eight further in Chapter 24.

Is it possible that our new perception of the existence of Calousia will also cause a revolutionary change in our view of our relationship with the universe? I've hinted at this. But let's see.

19

REVOLUTION #2: HOW DOES CALOUSIA'S EXISTENCE REVOLUTIONIZE OUR PERCEPTION OF OUR RELATIONSHIP WITH THE UNIVERSE?

Here is a **summary** of the revolutionary changes in our perception of our species' relationship with the universe, at least locally. This point must greatly strengthen our species' astonishing purpose.

Humanity's Place in the Advancing Universe's (AU's) Stage Six.

Heretofore, except as an abode for gods, the seeming cycle of the stars around us, the different cycles of the solar system entities, and the light energy from the sun, we were aware of no serious relationship between our human species and the great universe beyond. We therefore seemed both isolated and very different from all that "up there."

But now, as mentioned in Chapter 13, we know that **the universe, in the AU's Stages One through Six, made us**

humans. It first made the atoms of our bodies and then, through the universal processes of chemical evolution and biological evolution, it made our species, too.

More than that, we now know that **universal processes made us the Summit Species of the AU's Stage Six**. This is because it made us the first and only species on Earth able to improve itself over the generations through knowledge growth.

Compare us, for example, with dogs. An individual dog can learn an astonishing number of new things: tricks, words, reading the facial and bodily expressions of its owner, etc. But when this particular dog dies, all the extraordinary knowledge the dog acquired dies with it. It's lost, unavailable to other dogs. This condition is largely true for all other animals. We humans, however, being social, having spoken and written language, can keep accumulating and sharing the knowledge discovered by other humans, living and deceased.

This Stage Six Summit designation makes us humans a special universal species, the one among millions of earthly biological species that is crucial to the universe's advance. This new perception of ourselves as being created by universal processes, rather than just by local earthly processes, and being the Summit of Stage Six, is a major change in our perception of our relationship with the universe.

Humanity's Place in the AU's Stage Seven

Heretofore, we tended to think of ourselves as simply participating in Earth's biological progression. We tended to think that our superior genes and tools allowed us to do a better job than other animals in this kind of evolution on our planet.

But now we are aware that our Stage Seven progressive formula is a new kind of universal progression on Earth, a progression that's far faster and more purposeful than Stage Six's formula of mutations and selection. We are now also aware, from Chapter 13, that the summit material of one stage in the AU's history is automatically the starting material for the next stage, and that therefore we are the new material of the AU's Stage Seven. This new perception of ourselves is a major change in our perception of our relationship with the universe.

Is Calousian Creation a Universal Process?

Now we find ourselves participating in Stage Seven's new progressing process. How do we know that our long progression is a universal progression? After all, we have so far identified not one other example of this Great Progression in the entire universe. Several reasons.

First, as just noted, we now know that the summit entities of one AU stage are also the new material for the next stage.

Second, we know our Calousian-Creation Progression is a universal process, because although we are now aware that in our long progression, we do all the growing, universal conditions determine the results. This is because it's universal conditions that determine the maximizations and virtual maximizations of the three parts of us. For example, regarding the transportation ability, universal conditions determine the fastest possible travel speeds–the maximums.

That universal conditions determine our Stage Seven's Summit underscores our Calousian Creation as a universal process.

The third proof that our species' progression is a universal progression is the Calousian Mold, a way of looking at our Calousian-Creating Progression whole. The Calousian Summit here is the consequence of a process involving an expanding force (our species' increasing knowledge and abilities) meeting an immovable object (all the universe's limits to our growth).

Why does the Calousian Mold prove anything about Stage Seven being a universal process? It's because universal processes created both our species with its abilities-expanding character and the Summit-determining maximums to the benefits of Sci- Tech growth.

This answer, in part, is also a consequence of the principle of uniformity, which holds that what universal laws and conditions allow and forbid here, they will do the same for other, similar places and conditions elsewhere in the universe.

In consequence, **heretofore,** we viewed our long progression as simply the local activity that we humans involve ourselves in. **Now**, we know it's a universal process. This is yet another major change in our perception of our relationship with the universe.

Humanity's Place in Stage Seven's Calousian Summit

Heretofore, we didn't even know that our progression had a Summit. After all, if just the science part of SciTech is "an end-less frontier," perhaps we could just keep improving ourselves forever.

But now we are aware of this astonishing Stage Seven Calousian Summit. In a universe of possibly infinite growth of SciTech and other knowledge, what conditions could establish a place so distinctive and so elevated as to constitute the Summit of our long progression?

The answer, of course, is not that SciTech growth ends at Calousia. It doesn't. Instead it's because our SciTech growth finally completes our species' self-transcendence into the higher type of universal beings called Calousians.

This is true, first, because this future includes the maximization of our Seven Fundamental Abilities so important to our self- transformation. These maximized abilities are distinctive because of their high accomplishment and because, being maximized, they can never grow greater. In addition, this Summit future includes the virtual maximizing of our bodies and minds as we transcend into the distinctively far higher and more capable beings, called Calousians, beings who can thrive on local moons and planets, and on similar places far from their originating star. This future also includes the virtual maximizing of how Calousians live. In addition, this Calousian future is characterized by all the other knowledge and abilities accumulated up to this time.

Again, these maximizations and virtual maximizations do mark a distinctive place in the incessant growth of SciTech and other knowledge. Much more important, they mark a distinctive transformation of us ability-expanding humans, because at our Stage Seven's Summit, we humans will complete our self-transcendence into our mature Calousian condition. This Summit Stage distinguishes Calousians as superior to all the less advanced, biologically produced abilities expanders and as essentially equal to all Calousians, new or more advanced.

This new perception that our species plays a crucial role in the AU's Stage Seven, and that we fulfill it by maximizing our important abilities and virtually maximizing our bodies and minds and how we live, is still another major change in our perception of our relationship with the universe.

Humanity's Place as Stage Eight's New Material

Heretofore, we remained unaware that our species played any universal role at all.

But now we realize that we are the master creators of Calousians and Calousias and therefore also the maximizers of the Seven Fundamental Abilities and the virtual maximizers of Calousians and the ways Calousians live. In consequence, we now perceive that we humans have total responsibility for our species being successful in reaching our Stage Seven Summit.

If we succeed, our descendants, as Calousians, will be the special, crucial, universal Summit Species of the AU's Stage Seven. By the laws of our Great Progression, again, these descendants of ours, these new beings we will create, will also be the special, crucial, universal new product beings of the AU's Stage Eight. This major new view of our earthly human species transcending into Stage Seven Summit

Beings and therefore becoming Stage Eight's new material is an additional major change in perception from our previous view of our relationship with the universe.

Summary

Why does our knowledge of Calousia's existence revolutionize our perception of our relationship with the universe?

Because **heretofore**, the universe beyond the solar system seemed static, distant, and irrelevant to human lives, except as an abode of the gods.

Now we are aware that the universe is dynamic and vastly greater than previously imagined.

Regarding the creation of humans:

Heretofore, we thought the gods made us, or that our local biological evolution made us.

Now we accurately perceive that local aspects of universal conditions made us. Ancient stars created the atoms in our bodies. The AU's local Stage Five made many of our molecules and created life. The local Stage Six's biological evolution made our human bodies and minds.

Regarding our species' long progression:

Heretofore, we viewed it as just one of our species' many activities on our planet, and a minor one.

But now, though we have as yet no other universal examples of it, we can be sure that our long Great Progression is a most important universal process–the AU's Stage Seven. After all, the same stellar materials and similar conditions elsewhere among the two trillion galaxies might well, at their Stage Six's summit, produce ability-expanding beings who function very much the way that we humans do. During their Stage Sevens, some of these Pre-Calousians will also succeed in becoming Calousians. In other words, we become aware of the high probability that the progression we humans experience is a universal progression.

Regarding our species' universal role:

Heretofore, our species had none. The idea that we comparatively microscopic humans, in our busy local activities, play any significant role in the colossal universal realm was once unthinkable.

But now we perceive that our relationship to the AU is astonishingly intimate. We realize that we humans inescapably play crucial, essential universal roles in three of the AU's Seven or Eight known universal Stages. Yes, we now perceive that we are as essential to the Advancing Universe as stars. This is certainly a most revolutionary change in perception of our relationship to the AU. Furthermore, unlike stars whose AU influence is passive, our AU influence is aware, knowledgeable, deliberate, and organized. This, too, is a revolutionary change.

Regarding human individuals:

Heretofore, we individuals have had scarcely any influence on the laws or behavior of even our local nations.

But now, as noted previously, we realize that almost everything we individuals do–cooking, eating, disposing, bathing, having children, working, driving, etc.–on balance, either advances or retards our Calousian-Creation Progression. Therefore, we now realize, quite surprisingly, that our individual human relationship with the universe is both intimate and essential to the universe. This is because our individual activities, in total, determine whether the AU's Stage Seven here will be a success or failure. Yes, we now realize that **attaining the Summit is no longer a benefit just for us humans. It's for the AU, too**. This is unquestionably a revolutionary change in perception.

Regarding what we humans really are:

Heretofore, we viewed ourselves as mammal animals of the *Homo sapiens* type and also as tool users and culture bearers. We tended to see ourselves as members of particular nations, and perhaps localities–e.g., St. Petersburg, Russia; Shanghai, China; Belem, Brazil; and so on.

But now we realize that, in addition to the above categories, we are also Stage Six Summit beings. Furthermore, we are the new material for the AU's Stage Seven. In addition, we are the master creators of Stage Seven's Summit Calousias and Calousians. Finally, in this latter role, our descendants or those they create will also be the new material for the AU's Stage Eight. We now perceive, in sum, that we humans are significant, intimate, essential, big players in the Advancing Universe at least locally. This point must greatly strengthen our species' astonishing purpose.

In sum, we now know that the AU made us ability-expanding humans in Stages One through Six. It made the Calousian-Creating Process in Stage Seven that we participate in. It made the Stage Seven Summit of this process by determining limits to how much SciTech growth can keep expanding the three parts of us. And, finally, the universe will determine what's possible for those Calousian descendants of ours in Stage Eight.

All these extraordinary great differences between our past perceptions and our present ones regarding our relationship with the universe unquestionably constitute a revolutionary change in perception.

In Chapter Two, we took a first look at what we humans are. The answer then wasn't surprising. After all, we've known the answer for a long time. But in the next chapter, let's take a second look at what we are. Is it possible that learning of Calousia's existence could profoundly change our long-held, traditional view of even what we humans are? Let's see.

20

REVOLUTION #3: WHY DOES CALOUSIA'S EXISTENCE REVOLUTIONIZE OUR PERCEPTION OF US HUMANS?

It seems absurd, after all our species' many years of existence, to claim here that we humans have never really known what we are. But it's true. Let's see why.

Past View

In Chapter 2, we considered what humans are. We have traditionally identified ourselves as wise, i.e., as *Homo sapiens*, as culture bearers and tool users, all rather static categories. This static view of ourselves made sense to earlier classifiers, because that's the way they appropriately characterized all other forms of Earth life, as organisms that can't change, essentially, until their genes accidentally change.

But then we came to realize that we had advanced far from our hunt-and-gather origins, and that, since the potential growth of our knowledge seemed endless, we would probably keep advancing in knowledge, and consequently in how we live, far into the future.

Finally, since our species' bodies change only when groups of us are long isolated and only over periods of time far larger than our individual life-spans, we thought of ourselves as rather unchanging local beings of particular ancient heritages–e.g., French, Chinese, Spanish, African, American, etc. At the largest geographic scale, we thought of ourselves as earthly beings.

Present View

Now, how does our perception of **the existence of Calousia revolutionize our view of what we humans are?** Since we now think bigger and view our species in a larger perspective, it's reasonable that this new perspective would influence our view of what we humans are.

Now we realize that the more we learn, especially in the elementary and biological realms, the more certain we are that in the future we will safely acquire the capacity to improve parts of our minds and bodies. This capacity will in turn prompt us to make such changes, and to make ever more of them as our knowledge grows. It becomes apparent, then, that we are not, as we have tended to think, an essentially fixed, unchanging species. Instead, because of our capacity for knowledge and abilities growth, we now understand that we are, inherently, abilities expanders, a **self-improving, self-transforming species**.

But, of course, this self-transforming character of ours is **not yet evident** from what we have so far accomplished. That's because, until now, we've not deliberately made long-term changes in our bodies. What suggests our self-transforming character now is the accelerating growth of our knowledge of biology and other areas which, if we keep growing SciTech, must inevitably make that self-transforming knowledge available to us.

If we keep making ever more improvements in our bodies and minds, we must, in time, acquire the capacity to considerably transform ourselves. And the more we transform ourselves, the more we must **transcend** our original state. Therefore, we can now identify ourselves as a **potentially self-transcending species**. More precisely, we are mammal animals with the potential to self-transcend into the universal Calousian Summit Species of the Advancing Universe's, our AU's, Stage Seven.

Why are we humans inherently a self-transforming, self-transcending species? Again, it's because we have an inherent ability to keep expanding our abilities through knowledge growth over the generations. This is what enables and prompts us to keep changing and improving not just the world around us, but also our minds and bodies.

Now, as noted in the last chapter, we realize that our knowledge-acquiring, abilities-expanding character makes us not just unique on our planet, but also has made us the **Summit Species of the AU's Stage Six** here. In consequence, therefore, we also become the essential new material of the **AU's Stage Seven**. Remember, in Chapter 13, that the universe can advance only with the materials at hand. And as a consequence of this, we also become something quite new. Of necessity, we become the **essential managing material** for transforming and transcending ourselves into Calousians, the universal Summit species of the AU's Stage Seven. With this future self-transformation, we therefore also become, as Calousians, **the essential new material for the AU's Stage Eight**.

In sum, we no longer see ourselves as just earthly beings; instead, we perceive that we are the **key beings** for the universe's local advance, intimately involved in the AU's local progression through Stages Six, Seven, and Eight.

This progressive growth of ourselves is our **primary human characteristic**. It's the cause of our species' biggest and most important accomplishment, our long Great Progression.

This huge expansion of our perception of what we are is **unquestionably a revolutionary change**. It's also **essential,** because if we don't become aware of this more complete understanding of ourselves, we would lack the vision and therefore the purpose of completing ourselves at the Calousian Summit and progressing thereafter.

If our new knowledge of Calousia's existence changes our understanding of what we are from a fixed species to a self-transcending species, then what should we call ourselves?

Another Name

Wait a minute! We've already called ourselves, first, *Homo sapiens* and then abilities-expanders (see Chapter 2). Why do we need still another name?

We need another name because our *Homo sapiens* and abilities-expanders names are ways to distinguish ourselves from all Earth's other species. Calling ourselves abilities expanders is also a way to identify ourselves with a universal kind of species, assuming others exist, a species with the ability to keep increasing the kinds of things it can do and become over generations through knowledge growth. Therefore, the name abilities expanders makes sense.

Now, however, we need still another universal name for our species, one that reflects not just the starting point of our species' self-developing process, but its potential future mature, self-developed Summit state.

Such naming is not unusual. "Sapling" accurately identifies the young tree but is inadequate for the mature one. With humans, similarly, words like infant, child, youth, adolescent, and teenager accurately identify the young, but are inappropriate names for fully grown, mature adults.

So what universal name would appropriately identify us future technology-expanders?

As Chapter 11 suggests, isn't it **"Calousians,"** the condition toward which we are self-transcending? Isn't it **"Calousia,"** that state of mature abilities, that fulfillment of our species' potential, that chiefly defines our species?

Yes, and yes. But we are only potential Calousians, not yet Calousians. Therefore, let's call ourselves **"pre-Calousians."**

Again, remember that as we maximize our fundamental abilities, it's the universe–universal conditions–that will determine what our abilities will be at Calousia. Examples include, how fast we can travel and how much energy we have at our disposal. These universal conditions will also largely determine what our minds and bodies will be and how we will live in different parts of our galaxy at Calousia. This is because we will be making a sequence of rational adjustments to ourselves as our growing SciTech allows us to both better ourselves and better harmonize with the changes we make in our environments. Yes, the universe (universal conditions) is using us humans to create the higher universal beings called "Calousians."

What are "pre-Calousians"? Just as caterpillars transform themselves into butterflies, so we particular local abilities-expanders, we earthly pre-Calousians, have the inherent potential to self-transform into Calousians. But unlike caterpillars, whose genes transform them, we humans have total responsibility for our own advance, and must learn to successfully manage our own self-transformation and self-transcendence. In consequence, we "pre-Calousians" are more than potential Calousians; we are also, potentially, the **master creators of Calousians.**

Pre-Calousians and Calousians are typical components of the progressing universe, like atoms and stars. Except for their vast difference in their abilities, how do these two advanced intelligent components of the universe differ? Pre-Calousians arise from planets that may have quite different biologies, so pre-Calousians from different stars may differ widely from each other.

Calousians, in contrast, tend to be similar, because all are shaped not by local conditions, but by universal conditions. Universal conditions determine the Calousians' maximized fundamental abilities and consequently, since they are rational, much about the choices they make for their physical and mental character and how they live.

Summary

We are abilities expanders, a name that identifies us with those beings all over the universe, assuming they exist, who can grow their SciTech as we do. As abilities expanders, we will eventually acquire ever more ways to improve our fundamental abilities, our minds and bodies, and how we live. This means that we are also pre-Calousians, a self-transforming species with the potential to transcend its original mammal-animal, *Homo sapiens* state and become the higher universal beings called Calousians.

To succeed in this transformation, however, we human pre-Calousians must learn to fulfill a new role. As noted, we must become the master creators of our own self-transcendence into Calousians. This means, in turn, that we are not only the master creators of the AU's Stage Seven's Summit, but we are also, therefore, the master creators of the new Calousian material for the AU's Stage Eight, assuming such a stage exists.

Yes, the existence of Calousia causes a revolutionary change in our perception of what we humans are. We now perceive that we are a bigger and more extraordinary species than we heretofore thought. And this new awareness of Calousia has caused a revolutionarily change in our perception of the nature and future of our species.

How does our perception of the existence of Calousia influence human purpose? This question will be answered in the next chapter.

21

WHY DOES CALOUSIA'S EXISTENCE GIVE OUR SPECIES A PRIMARY PURPOSE?

In Chapter 16, I mentioned that our awareness of the Calousian Summit's existence gave our species, for the first time in human existence, a primary purpose. This was part of this book's Revolution #1. But let's now look a little further at this revolutionary primary purpose.

As noted, our species is chiefly defined by our knowledge-accumulating, self-transforming, Calousian-Creation condition. Now, if the universe, through its laws and conditions, allows our species to progress to this higher Calousian Summit existence, this fulfillment of our potential, then isn't it also, in a sense, **giving our species the purpose** of reaching this Calousian goal?

Local aspects of universal laws and conditions give an apple seed the purpose of becoming an apple tree, a chicken egg the purpose of becoming a chicken, and a human fetus the purpose of becoming an human adult. Can't we say, then, that these universal laws and conditions also give our species the purpose of becoming Calousian?

It may at first surprise you, as it did me, but the answer to this question is "yes." When we become aware that Calousia exists, we also realize that this potential future prompts a new and imperative primary role for every member of our species: it's to reach Calousia.

Why?

Three Reasons For Our Primary Purpose

Here are three reasons why reaching Calousia is the primary purpose of our species.

1. It's Hugely Beneficial to Ourselves

The **first reason** is because of all the benefits this purpose provides. To make these benefits clear, let's look at two snap-shots of human existence, each reflecting the amount of SciTech available. The first snapshot shows our original way of living, the second how we live today.

Snapshot From 12,000 Years Ago

Imagine that you were born some 12,000 years earlier and that you find yourself living as an ancient Aborigine in central Australia. You are typically homeless because you live by hunting and gathering the food nature provides, and since you soon exhaust the easy-to-find local supply, you and your group must keep moving to fresh territory.

This constant moving means you can own only what you can conveniently carry. As a woman, you carry about twelve pounds of equipment, including a wooden bowl, cooking tools, a digging stick, and perhaps a flint knife. As a man, you carry a shield, a spear and spear-thrower, a boomerang, and a stone ax, the latter often hanging on a belt made from the hair of your mother-in-law.

Having neither home nor clothing, at night you sleep naked and uncovered on the ground, perhaps on some gathered leaves. On very cold nights you sleep close to a small fire you've made.

You are intelligent and a sophisticated hunter and gatherer, but your extremely low SciTech provides scant understanding of the world. You think the sun is a woman; the moon is a man; Orion, the constellation, is an emu, an ostrich-like bird; and all of these astronomical entities stay nearby when not in the sky. Almost all stars are campfires, but certain ones are malignant brothers who kill the very ill by pinching their throats. All the physical aspects of your environment–for example, its hills, distinctive rocks, water holes, and caves–exist as a consequence of the activities of ancestral spirit beings. Animals, plants, and humans exist because spirits enter them–and when these spirits leave, the living die.

Not understanding procreation, having sex and the conception of a child are two quite separate activities. Your father is not the man living with your mother; in your particular case, your father is a kangaroo. Fathers are those ancestral spirits who take many forms. Your mother identified your father as a kangaroo because one of these animals happened by when she first felt you in her abdomen. One consequence of this parentage is that you cannot eat kangaroo meat.

If you suffer an illness or injury, the cause is always due to the magic practiced by a human or a spirit. A sinister consequence is that a death often causes the additional deaths of the quite innocent whose magic is suspected to have been the cause.

Your language names only three specific colors: red, white, and black. You use the same word for green, blue, and yellow.

As a man or women you enhance yourself with a bone through the nose, often a kangaroo thighbone. In addition, you wear scars on your chest made by flint-knife cuts followed by rubbed in ashes. As a woman, to be particularly attractive you might knock out a front tooth.

You are lighthearted, but anxiety lies just beneath. This is because you see your world as operating not by laws, but governed haphazardly by spirits, some of which are mercurial and good; however, most spirits are bad. You attempt to gain their help or avoid the dangers they can inflict by spending much of your time participating in ceremonies, obeying traditions, and practicing magic.

This morning, while you sat naked on the dusty ground and the gusting wind blew sand in your eyes, the paint-smeared, wild-haired witch doctor/shaman danced and chanted about you, using his magic to "cure" that deep bite in your throbbing, festering leg. Being so injured, you wonder how you would find and kill your next meal.

Snapshot of Today

Now think of your advantageous life today, if you are lucky enough to live this way: You wear clothing of many different kinds, including hats and shoes, depending on your activities and the weather. Your home is automatically heated and cooled, with lights brightened or dimmed, and perhaps turned on and off automatically. You sleep on a bed hardened or softened to taste. Your kitchen may contain a gas or electric stove, a microwave oven, a refrigerator, instant hot or cold water, a garbage disposal, and a dishwasher.

Appliances automatically wash and dry your clothes. If you plan to travel, you use a car or fly in an airplane. Your doctors and hospitals provide real cures to help you live a longer and more healthful life, and you enjoy many kinds of entertainments, such as 3-D color TVs, movies, cellphones, sports events, theaters, symphonies, art galleries, dance halls, and clubs.

Supermarkets exemplify your advantages today compared with your distant ancestor. The average supermarket carries over 39,000 items. These include all kinds of meat and poultry you don't have to kill and dress yourself, fish you don't have to catch, and milk without the care of a cow. They offer butter, fresh-baked bread and delicious pastries, and many kinds of fresh fruits and vegetables so easy to pick up. They provide frozen dinners, and, even in midwinter, fresh-frozen strawberries and peas all year round, and flowers flown in from warmer regions.

Furthermore, the supermarket's delis sell ready-to-eat salads and cheese and meat dishes, following tasty recipes that call for herbs, rich spices, and condiments. You can buy beverages (plain and carbonated), beer, ale, wine, and higher alcoholic drinks, along with snacks, assorted candies, and desserts, including ice cream.

Indeed, the food available to the average supermarket customer of today far surpasses what was available even to kings a hundred years ago.

This is one of many ways that our growing technological knowledge has expanded the scope of individual existence.

The distance from our first example, the primitive hunting-and-gathering way of life, to the second example of how many people live today, illustrates the impressive progress our species has made. It's the consequence of our increasing store of SciTech that allows us to do ever more kinds of things. It's an abilities-expanding process. And it tends to accelerate, moving ever faster.

This accelerating change can lead to Calousia i.e., "beautiful existence." And again, the name is not meant to indicate a utopia, but rather to characterize a distinctive, dazzling, high-capacity future that fulfills our species' potential.

If, somehow, we could see Calousians now, exercising their mature abilities, they would seem magical to us, just as we would seem magical to our primitive hunting and gathering ancestors of 12,000 years ago if they could see us now.

Yes, Calousia offers us the biggest, richest, best-possible future.

It is vastly superior to our present condition, and getting there would fulfill our species' extraordinary potential.

So the **first** reason that reaching Calousia is our species' primary purpose is because of all the benefits this purpose can provide. These include the maximum benefits at Calousia itself, and the increasing benefits to all of us as we advance to Calousia, as we keep expanding the scope of individual human existence, providing each generation with greater benefits, such as a longer, healthier, broader, and richer existence. No other purpose provides comparable advantages.

Another advantage to this primary purpose is that reaching Calousia is doable and potentially near, most of it being, if we advance properly, only about 200 years away.

Still a **further advantage** to striving toward Calousia is that it gives us hope that our species can create and enjoy ever-better futures as we strive for the best future of all. And now that we are aware of the necessary method for this hope, which is to keep growing SciTech and to keep adjusting rationally to the resulting changes, we have the means to more certainly transform this hope into reality.

In sum, the first reason reaching Calousia is humanity's primary goal is that no other goal offers the individual or our species comparable benefits. And none offer us a more realistic hope for a far better future, as well as the means to make this hope a reality. Acquiring these mature benefits is reason enough to strive for Calousia.

2. Reaching Calousia Expresses Our True Character

The **second reason** that reaching Calousia is the primary purpose of our species, and therefore of all humans, derives, as noted in Chapter 20, from our basic character. We are inherently knowledge accumulators, **ability-expanders**, beings who can increase the kinds of things they can do over the generations through knowledge growth. This is why we find ourselves participating in Calousian Creation.

Because of our abilities-expanding character, the more knowledge we acquire, the more we can improve ourselves. Therefore, we are potentially a **self-transforming, self-transcending species.** Like fish learning to swim or birds to fly, this self-transforming ability expresses what is most significant and unique in us. Moving toward Calousia expresses our species' unique character; reaching Calousia fulfills our species' potential.

Note that our Calousian-Creation advance, unlike that of all Earth's other species, does not depend upon accidental genetic mutations and natural selection. After all, we will soon be able to deliberately improve any of our genes that we choose to. Our advance depends upon our deliberate and persistent acquisition of SciTech knowledge, upon the social accumulation of this knowledge and upon our rational adjustment to the resulting changes.

In sum, the second reason that reaching Calousia is humanity's primary purpose is because in striving for Calousia we most express our species' unique character. In getting there **we most fulfill our species' astonishing potential.**

3. Reaching Calousia Reflects Our Species' Key AU Role

The **third reason** that reaching Calousia is our primary purpose derives from our **species' special position** in the progressive evolution of the universe. In other words, it derives from that evolutionary advance from the Big Bang's fiercely hot plasma to galaxies, stars, and planets, and then to single and multicellular life, and thereafter on up to humans and potentially up to Calousians.

We are the most advanced species in the solar system, the high product of billions of years of biological evolution on our planet, of life reproducing, mutating, growing, multiplying, and dying. But as noted, we are not just the high product of biological evolution; we are that evolution's Summit species.

This means that we are the Summit entities not only of the entire solar system but also of part of our galaxy as well. We don't yet know where the nearest abilities-expanders and Calousians are, so we don't yet know the breadth of our region of evolutionary preeminence. But we do know that relative to Earth, it's enormous.

Our species therefore plays an **intimate role in the progressing universe.** Perhaps the best proof of this is that as we maximize our abilities and ourselves, it's the universal conditions revealed by the universal Calousian mold, that determine the abilities and character of the higher, Calousian, universal beings that we become. As we advance ourselves, we are at the same time also advancing our part of the evolving, progressing universe. To put it another way, we in our progression do the growing; the universe, by setting limits, determines what we will be at the summit. The main line of the local universe's progressive development runs through our kind, though our veins.

And if we help our species fulfill its potential and reach Calousia, then those mature high-capacity beings that we create may play an even higher role in the further evolution of the universe.

Yes, we humans now realize that we are intimately connected to the AU. If the AU is to succeed in its Stage Seven here, **we are the ones who must do it.** Again, we are as important to the AU as stars and planets. And everything each of us individual humans does, on balance, either helps our species succeed or hinders it.

What again is our species' astonishing purpose? It's to self- transcend into the higher Calousian beings, the new material, that the AU needs at the start of its Stage Eight.

When our Calousian Creation is viewed from this larger perspective, reaching Calousia is much more than our species' primary purpose. It's the biggest, most important activity of our species. Succeeding in this activity is our sacred duty.

Summary

Reaching Calousia is our species' astonishing primary purpose for three reasons. First, no other goal offers our species, now and in the future, comparable benefits or hope. This is more than enough reason to reach Calousia. Second, striving for Calousia fully expresses and makes use of our species' abilities-expanding, self-transforming character. Third, our species is the crucial, most advanced part of the local universe's progressive evolution. In consequence, whether the universe continues its progressive advance locally–and conceivably throughout the entire cosmos–depends upon our species; it depends upon what we do.

All this knowledge, these new perceptions of ourselves, of our purpose in fulfilling our inherent potential, and of our role in the AU, should powerfully motivate us to succeed in our Calousian Creation role. And, obviously, without this motivation, reaching Calousia becomes impossible.

Can the existence of the Calousian Summit change our perception of our cultures, races, and nations? It doesn't seem probable, does it? The next chapter will look into this question.

22

REVOLUTION #4: HOW DOES CALOUSIA'S EXISTENCE REVOLUTIONIZE OUR PERCEPTION OF RACES, CULTURES, AND NATIONS?

Basic Point: Because of our abilities-expanding character–i.e., our being able to learn and create new things and accumulate this and other knowledge socially–all of us humans participate **in one and the same Great Progression, the Calousian-Creation process**. In other words, we are now increasingly aware that all of us humans work, so to speak, for the same Calousian-Creation Corporation.

This new truth that all of us exist primarily in the same Calousian-Creating process must radically change how we think of races, cultures, and nations.

These three entities have long been with us, long been of considerable importance in our day-to-day lives. It's very difficult, therefore, to imagine them radically changing in the near future.

But that's what will happen. Why? As you will see, it's because compared with the Calousian Creation process, races, cultures, and nations are the temporary consequences of temporary levels of SciTech and temporary adjustments thereto, so as Calousian Creation advances, these three designations must lose ever more significance.

Races

Races are the oldest of these three categories. All humanity started as dark-skinned individuals, whose advantageous melanin protected them from the African sun. But humans, being highly mobile, tend to wander. And as small groups of humans moved off to new distant places, they became isolated. They bred among themselves and no longer with the larger group they had left. In time, under new conditions and reflecting the differences in their group's starting genes and the differences in their mutations acquired during isolation, they became new races.

But now, modern communication and transportation technologies shrink distances ever more, causing us to trend toward one global society. Isolation is disappearing. Mating among individuals of different races tends to produce more and more individuals of mixed race, a tendency that promises to continue, and probably accelerate.

Much more important, growing SciTech is giving us increasing control over our genes. In consequence, in the future, nearer than most suspect, parents are going to be able to choose any racial features they want in their newly conceived children.

In addition, as we advance toward the Summit, more and more children will be born with corrected genes, and later with improved genes, and still later with advanced genes. As children all over the planet are born with the same ever-more advanced genes, they will tend to become a different species, quite different from what we humans are today. Eventually, if we are adequate to the task, all of us will progress to becoming Calousians.

In sum, as we look over our long Stage Seven progression, we understand how races started and developed, and how they are bound to diminish in the future. As we approach Calousia, all parents will be making similar improvements in their offspring and getting closer to becoming Calousians. Eventually, all present races will disappear. In this sense, today's races are a temporary condition. To the extent that they cause problems between peoples, they are a disappearing problem.

Cultures

Cultures are the second oldest of this chapter's three categories. Cultures, too, began with wandering and with the resulting isolation, which allowed the formation of distinctive new languages and ways of living.

Our Great Progression–our species' biggest achievement, this astonishing growth of our knowledge and our adjustments to this knowledge–has advanced through stages. **Stage 1**, hunting and gathering, i.e., living off the foods that nature supplies, is by far the longest stage. The ancestors of all humans began this way. **Stage 2**, the agricultural revolution, raising plants and animals, began about 11,000 years ago. **Stage 3**, the urban revolution, the advance from tribal villages and small towns to cities, began around 5,000 years ago. The much larger population here is the consequence of better farming techniques in advantageous environments. **Stage 4**, the industrial revolution, began around 1760 when small-scale production by individuals in their homes changed to large-scale production by many workers in factories powered by steam engines burning coal. **Stage 5**, our modern world, characterized by great growth of knowledge, electric power, airplanes, rocket ships, phones, computers, the creation of mega-cities, etc.

It follows that those living in these different Stages of our Calousian-Creation Progression, as they adjust to their different levels of knowledge in different environments, will create different cultures.

The problem is that not all humans have progressed through all our Great Progression's Stages. A diminishing number of us still remain hunters and gatherers. An example is the Parahã of the Maici River in the Amazon, who can walk into the jungle naked, with no tools or weapons, and walk out three days later with baskets of fruit, nuts, and small game, according to anthropological linguist Daniel Everett. Many more around the world continue to live their lives as early farmers, i.e., subsistence farmers, eating what their family grows. And many, many more, mostly because of where they live, have been unable to enjoy the full benefits of our **Stage 5** modern world.

In the recent past the tendency has been to see those in our modern world who cling to primitive cultures based on inferior SciTech, as individuals who have just chosen to retain ancient ways. And this choice has often been respected. In the U.S., for example, native American tribes have been given lands, and considerable independence and self-governance.

Why have some of these primitive, indigenous cultures around the world **not advanced** to our modern world? Part of the answer is their being in isolated places. Part of it is their tribal cultures, often built around family relationships, which have kept them isolated. Part of it is tradition, their clinging to what they have long known. Part of it is that these traditional conditions and values give them their sense of identity. And part of it is that our modern world adaptations to SciTech, being far from perfect, have not attracted them. Think again of our relentless environmental destruction, and our many intercontinental missiles carrying nuclear weapons.

But why, now, should members of these indigenous cultures change?

First, because they now know of the Calousian Summit, and therefore that all of us humans participate in one and the same great Calousian-Creation Progression.

Second, this progression makes evident the new view of **what we humans are**. We realize now that we are not a static species, because our growing knowledge keeps expanding our abilities and therefore what we are. We are Earth's first and only self-developing, self-expanding, and therefore self-transforming species. This exciting new view is missing in primitive cultures.

Third, the above new facts reveal that if we keep growing, we can eventually reach the much **bigger, better Summit** world. So although primitive cultures based upon modest STEMM knowledge could create our species first course, these cultures are too out-of-date to help us enjoy the full-course banquets of Calousians.

Fourth, yes, small living examples of particular indigenous cultures allow us to educate ourselves about our past, and so should be maintained. But we of the modern world need those continuing to live in less advanced ways to change, so that they can **help us advance** and adjust to the Great Progression's fast-changing conditions ahead.

Fifth, those persisting in ancient cultures can't really escape the influence of our modern world, because our trains, airplanes, intruders, diseases, climate change, and environmental degradation will affect them, too. In addition, our SciTech knowledge will continue its rapid growth and our one great Calousian-Creation Progression will continue its accelerating advance. In consequence, all the **indigenous cultures may fade into irrelevance**. Therefore, individuals who continue to pursue these old ways will find themselves confined to less meaningful lives, alien to the progressions of both our species and our advancing universe.

Sixth, we are not asking tribal and indigenous people to raise themselves up to where we moderns are. After all, we moderns are not Calousians, either. In truth, all of us humans must grow and change if we are to succeed in our one, great, fast-changing and increasingly complex Calousian-Creation environment and reach its Calousian Summit. And in this great task we need the help of everyone.

We see that as we progress, as our SciTech grows and changes, our economies and societies will change, and many of our descendants will live on moons and planets beyond Earth. Those who remain here will eventually form one predominant earthly language and culture. Yes, it will contain fragments of many present and earlier cultures, but it must also be larger and quite different from any former cultures.

Cultures are a response to what we are, what we know, and to our environment, and in our Calousian-Creating Progression all these components will greatly change. Yes, we humans cannot any longer see ourselves as just static culture bearers. Instead, we are also the creators, expanders, and destroyers of cultures.

City-States and Nations

Nations are the newest of the three categories considered here. Their city-state predecessors began around 5,000 years ago in the area between the Tigris and Euphrates rivers in present-day Iraq. Tribal territories preceded them. City-states and nations have territories, leaders to govern them, and smaller component organizations (tax collectors, armed forces, etc.) supporting their work. Leaders must defend their territories, maintain order, and, hopefully, improve the wellbeing of their people.

Today, nations are our planet's primary social organizations. Many citizens consider their primary allegiance to be to their nation.

But as our large-scale Calousian-Creation Progression advances, it must alter our perception of nations, too. In fact, nations are **already losing power** and adequacy. SciTech growth, by greatly improving our transportation and communication skills, continues to hugely shrink the world. Many problems nations face can now only be solved at the global level. Examples include climate change, viral and bacterial pandemics, and the horrendous power of new weapons. This loss of full control over problems they face necessarily weakens nations.

In consequence, nations are joining together to solve these problems, for example, the European Union and the United Nations (UN). Organizations associated with the UN are growing in importance as they fight pandemics and climate change and provide international security.

But as Calousian-Creation progresses, nations must lose ever more primacy. The territory we humans live on will greatly expand as we create human settlements and larger organizations in extraterrestrial places–e.g., the moon, Mars, and more distant sites. And just as the early independent principalities within present-day Germany, Russia, and Italy lost power and stopped fighting each other when they aggregated into their larger national states, so in the future, our present earthly nations will have their boundaries adjusted and will no longer fight each other when incorporated into the larger, future, world-wide and multi-astral community.

As for the Chinese nation, it, too, was once a collection of independent, warring principalities. Then Qin Shi Huangdi united these principalities into a great nation. But eventually this grand consolidation fell apart, and the territorial fragments fell under rule by Britain, Japan, and other nations. Now the Chinese have consolidated again and have grown to become the planet's second biggest economy. This is an amazing achievement.

But the world of China's past greatness is gone, too. They can't conquer again all their former territory any more than other nations–such as Britain, the U.S., Nederlands, Portugal, or the city of Rome–can recapture all their former territories.

It's becoming increasingly obvious to all now that **we cannot continue our long tradition of wars with ever-more powerful weapons**. Remember today's weapons are a thousand times more powerful than the two that ended the Second World War. Our weapons have become so powerful that they now truly threaten our human existence. We must give up this long tradition of nations acquiring other nations' territories through war. We don't need the incinerated world that hyper-nationalism promises. We don't need leaders, perhaps grown emotionally and mentally ill by being too long in power, to start meaningless, unnecessary wars. These old ways, these old demonstrations of power, have become both too meaningless and too destructive.

More important, our world has greatly changed. Nations still have their importance. But with our new knowledge of the existence of Calousia, the **primary environment** of all of us humans on Earth must increasingly become less and less individual nations and, as you will see in the next chapter, more and more our fast-changing and increasingly complex Calousian-Creation environment itself.

Finally, if nations are going to lose their present dominance in the not-too-distant future, let's use this knowledge to prevent their fighting now. Let's employ that considerable warring and defensive energy and money, instead, to reaching the highly advantageous Calousia, and to reach it sooner and more certainly for everyone.

In other words, instead of self-destructive competition, we need a world-wide cooperation that produces a world-wide management, which encourages all peoples to contribute what they can as we deliberately strive for our biggest, richest, best-possible future for all at the Calousian Summit.

Summary

Races, cultures, and nations appear important to us today. But we should take the present importance of all three of these categories with a grain of salt.

So if, in our Calousian Creation Progression, races, cultures, and nations lose prominence, what areas, if any, gain prominence? The answer to that is found in the next chapter.

23

REVOLUTION #5: HOW DOES CALOUSIA'S EXISTENCE REVOLUTIONIZE OUR PERCEPTION OF OUR PRIMARY ENVIRONMENT?

Our Past Perception

As we have previously noted, for ages our species did not progress. And even when it started progressing–during the Agricultural Revolution, some 11,000 years ago, and the Urban Revolution, some 5,000 years ago–our progression was so slow and took place over so many generations, that it was hardly noticed. It just seemed that some people chose one way of life–hunting and gathering–and others, another way–farming or running small shops.

Early on, tribal individuals and local groups probably viewed their primary environment, if they thought of it at all, as their natural environment. Later, their natural environment meant their families, farms, small businesses, small towns, friends and associates, and the local mix of natural and man-made environments.

And this environmental view didn't change much through Ancient Greek times. By Roman times, the environment also included empires. But certainly by the **Industrial Revolution**, in the early 1700s, inventions, such as new ways to make iron, the steam engine, widespread use of coal energy, and great factories making large quantities of product, made our species' long self-improvement increasingly evident. Of course, the primary environment for individuals remained the family home, friends, and associates, but it now included the nation, the factory, its income, its environment and people, and the larger industrial city, or at least their part of that city.

Nevertheless, our species' long progression still remained too slow and too distant from individual lives for practical consideration.

Now, we know that SciTech is the primary knowledge of our long progression, but this fact, at first, changed our perception of our primary environment only modestly. This is because people like the wise **Vannevar Bush**, science advisor to Presidents **Roosevelt** and **Truman**, called science "an endless frontier." It therefore seemed that science and our human progression could keep advancing forever.

So the perception of our species' long progression has been a factor in our recent human lives, but it has been far from our primary environment. Certainly it was not as important to us individuals as our local natural and social environments, nor as important as our nations, economies, and businesses. And virtually no one considered our species' progression important enough to deserve a serious major planet-wide managerial effort. Why? In part, because no one saw any distinct, particular future to strive towards.

Our Present Perception

Most people today would probably still say that their primary environment is their family, local community, business, and nation. Some might say it's "Earth." But our perception of our primary environment will soon greatly change.

For one thing, we will no longer view our primary environment as static or slow-advancing.

We used to think that if we stayed still, for example, sat down quietly in an overstuffed chair, we were not moving at all. Now we know this is not true. If our chair is near the equator, we are spinning with Earth at about a thousand miles an hour (Earth at equator = 4,000; 2PiR = 2 x 3.14 x 4,000 =25,120 miles divided by 24 hours = ca 1,000 mph). Furthermore, since our planet also races around the sun, while still in the overstuffed chair, we are now also speeding at almost an additional 66,000 mph (For circuit around the sun: 2PiR = 2 x 3.14 x 92 million = 577,760,000 divided by 365 = 1,580,000 miles per day; divided by divided by 24 = 65,833 mph). Then there's our even more rapid speed of 496,800 mph as our sun circles our galaxy (It's 828,000 km per hour, or about 496,800 mph, distance to moon ca 240,000 miles, so at that speed you could fly to the moon in 30 minutes). And finally, Andromeda approaches us at 244,800 mph, so if half of that is our galaxy's speed, we'd be moving in this direction at 122,400 mph.

Therefore, yes, while still lounging comfortably in that chair, we now know that our environment's apparent lack of motion is far from the truth. During those times when Earth is spinning, moving around the sun, running around our galaxy, and our galaxy is moving toward Andromeda, i.e., when all these motions happen to move in the same direction, this means that we are really traveling at some 685,200 mph. Hold tight! That's breathtaking! Isn't it? But it's still quite slow compared to the 669,600,000 mph speed of light. (Note: This chapter may be the most moving of the entire book.)

We are now also aware that our species' progression is advancing increasingly faster and becoming increasingly complex because more individuals and institutions are focusing on SciTech. Our social and economic environments also become more complex because increasing SciTech adds new abilities, creates more specialists and more kinds of goods and services, and these make the economy and the society increasingly complex. How different today is compared to the simpler, slow-advancing earlier times when everyone either hunted and gathered or, later, farmed!

Furthermore, these environmental changes are increasingly **planet-wide.** Transportation and communication growth are producing a global society and economy. Examples of this new planet-wide condition include climate change, with its floods, hurricanes, droughts, and rising sea levels; environmental degradation, with its species extinctions, loss of forests, and pollution of both land and seas; diseases, like the spread of Covid; the spread of weapons of increasing destruction; and, finally, the increasingly dangerous competitions between nations–e.g., the U.S. and China–all taking place on a global scale.

And now more and more people are learning, for the first time, that our fast-changing, accelerating, increasingly complex Great Progression has a natural, universal,

Calousian Summit, a future condition far superior to how we live today.

As noted, knowledge of our long Great Progression's Summit tells us that our primary environment will no longer be our tribes, cultures, races, or national governments. These components of our species' long progression will grow ever less important as our Great Progression advances. Regarding races, as noted, with DNA control, people can soon choose for their new children any racial characteristic they desire.

Knowledge of the Summit **empowers us** to begin our **deliberate advance** toward this Summit, and this will cause us to enter the exciting, increasingly progressive last stage of Calousian Creation. This is the period that begins when we first become aware of Calousia's existence and ends when we finally reach the Summit. In this last stage, we will develop SciTech knowledge much faster, causing our social, economic, and environmental conditions to be not only **ever-faster changing,** but **increasingly complex,** with new products, services, and conditions, as we advance toward the Summit.

In this new, more complex environment, we must **adjust** ever faster and on an ever larger scale. As noted in Chapter 16, everything we individuals around the Earth do, on balance, either advances or delays our advance to Calousia. This means that once we enter this fast-changing, increasingly complex last stage of Calousian Creation, **almost every decision** that individuals, groups, and governments make must take into account that particular decision's influence on our success in Calousian Creation.

In addition, we will soon realize that to be successful, we must begin **managing** our advance.

All these changes and new knowledge will finally begin to create a **revolutionary change in our perception of our primary environment**. We will begin to understand that in this last stage of Calousian Creation, the primary environment for all humans will soon become our new Calousian Creation progression itself.

Why will Calousian Creating become our most important environment? It's because, to be successful, it will be the main environment that all parts of humanity–individuals, groups, governments, and our entire species–must keep adjusting to. This is obviously a revolutionary change in both perception and in reality. And, of course, how we adjust to this new environment will determine whether we humans will ultimately fail or succeed in our primary Great Progression.

Again, Why Is This New Perception of Our Primary Environment Revolutionary?

I'll give two reasons. The first is because this new Calousian Creating Progression (CCP) environment will be so different than in the past.

1. It's Revolutionary Because It's So Different

It's different in **purpose.** Heretofore, our species had no particular purpose, as different groups and individuals wandered in different directions. Now, knowledge of the Summit will increasingly unite us in the purpose to reach this superior future condition that benefits all humans.

It's different in **size.** Heretofore, as noted, the environments that humans considered primary tended to be local, static, and rather simple. Now, for the first time, we realize that the primary environment we are entering is planet-wide, and perhaps solar-system wide, and that it will include all humans–from individuals, to groups, to our entire species.

It's different in its **speed of change**. Previously, our important environments tended to appear essentially static. From now on, our increasingly planet-wide environment will be not just fast-changing and complex, but these characteristics will accelerate.

It's different in being **inclusive.** Heretofore, different individuals and groups experienced different primary environments. Now our Calousian Creating Progression is becoming the primary environment of all humans: individuals, groups, and our entire species. It's obviously primary for our species because if we don't succeed in our progression, our species will fail its AU Stage Seven task. All humanity will fail to fulfill its astonishing potential. It's obviously primary for us human individuals, too. This is because the CCP is the main reality we must begin to adjust to if we hope to avoid failure and continue to prosper. As noted, virtually everything we individuals do, on balance, either advances or retards our progressive evolution. It's clear, therefore, that all human individuals must participate intimately in our new universal CCP environment, in this latter part of the AU's Stage Seven.

It's different in its **complexity.** The CCP includes the complex changes in our natural environments, and those in our world-wide economy and society, and in the people of different cultures as they advance toward the one and the same Calousian-Summit goal.

The CCP is different not only in being perceived as a human progression, but as a **human progression with a**

particular, specific Summit future. Once we realize the Calousian Summit exists, this new environment will undergo accelerating change. It's a consequence of the accelerating growth of SciTech and other knowledge, of the growth of our many abilities, of the improvements in our bodies and minds, and of the resulting changes in our planet-wide society and economy and in how we will live.

These differences from the past are revolutionary. They are overwhelming. And there is **a second big reason** why this new environmental perception is revolutionary.

2. It's Revolutionary Because It Requires Large-Scale Management

Now that we realize that we're in an accelerating progression, a Calousian-Creating Progression, a new kind of primary environment, we also realize that to succeed in it, we can't proceed as before. As we have noted, our small-scale nations and cultures are becoming increasingly inadequate to this much larger task. We can't continue our helter-skelter adjusting to the accelerating changes ahead. We need a new approach, an organized approach. In other words, as noted in Chapter 16, we need to persistently manage our accelerating, global progression. And this, too, is a revolutionary new situation in human affairs.

Why must this new primary environment be managed?

The answer is because history shows that big, complex projects must be managed to succeed. Our Calousian Creation Progression project is the biggest, most complex task we humans have ever taken. It's too fast-changing, too increasingly complex, too new, too important, and too difficult to succeed in without management. Persistent management is the essential way to succeed in our accelerating Calousian-Creating primary environment. It's the best way to help our human lives become ever richer and better, and it will help us and our children enjoy the increasing advantages as we progress ever nearer the Calousian Summit and eventually reach it.

Persistent management will also help us avoid dangerous wrong directions such as continuing climate change, population surges, and the use of weapons of ever-increasing destructiveness.

Finally, persistent management is the essential, rational means for adjusting to the accelerating changes in our accelerating primary environment. If we don't take this managerial step, our mis-adjustments to the accelerating speed and complexity of our primary Calousian-Creating environment are far more likely to take us suddenly down to extinction, than up to the Calousian Summit.

Note that this large-scale management is not an entirely new idea. After World War One, nations cooperated in creating the League of Nations. And after World War Two, they formed the better organized United Nations. So the need to organize ourselves on a world-wide scale to tackle our increasing number of world-wide problems is not new. In fact, our present task is simply the appropriate extension and improvement of an activity already begun and improved. Our organization and management just have to be expanded and improved far more.

This persistent global management of our progression will be revolutionary because our species has never really assumed this crucial responsibility before.

Why Is This New Primary-Environment Perception Essential?

The answers are: because without this new perception that our Calousian-Creating Progression is our primary environment, we would **continue to underestimate** both our progression's importance and the crucial role therein of each human individual. Again, almost everything we individuals do influences our species' advance, on balance, positively or negatively.

Because without this new perception, we would be far less likely to see or appreciate the importance of the **Summit**, or be willing to strive for it.

Because without new perception, we would be unlikely to comprehend that reaching this Calousian Summit is the biggest, most complex and fastest-changing task that we individuals have ever faced. As a result, we would not see the resulting necessity of our **taking charge** of this newly important progression and of managing our way forward. Yes, it's true that none of the AU's previous Stages needed organization or management. That's because none had or needed a multitude of independent acting, thinking, and learning components.

Because without this new perception, we'd be reluctant to make the unusually **great effort** required to create the big, new, world-wide management organizations essential to reaching the Calousian Summit.

Because without this new perception, we would still think that particular conditions, or nations, or some other entities were our primary environment, and so we would probably continue choosing wrong directions until it was too late, as we are threatening to do now with overpopulation, climate change, and wars with ever more powerful weapons.

Because without this new perception, we would essentially remain a **lost**, ineffective species, prone to self-destruction.

In sum, the idea that the primary environment for both us as individuals and for our species will soon be our complex, fast-changing, planet-wide Calousian-Creating Progression is **revolutionary**. But this change in perception is more than revolutionary; it's the **essential environment that we must adjust to**. Without forming this new perception, our species cannot succeed in reaching the Calousian Summit, the primary goal for both ourselves and the Advancing Universe.

Reaching Calousia, if we can get there at all, appears to take us a very, very long time into the future. Does it? And is there an AU Stage Eight? These answers lie just ahead in the next chapter.

24

HOW FAR AWAY IS CALOUSIA? DOES THE AU HAVE A STAGE EIGHT?

Considering all we must learn to reach Calousia–maximizing the three parts of us, adjusting to the accelerating changes, etc.– it seems reasonable that this potential Calousia ahead of us is as high above our present condition as our present condition is above that of our primitive hunt-and-gather ancestors.

So if it has taken some 12,000 years–at the minimum, since our hunt-and-gather life started some 300,000 years ago–to get from hunting and gathering to the advantageous life many enjoy today, it seems reasonable, since we have so much still to learn, to think that reaching Calousia will take (at a minimum) another 12,000 years.

But this isn't true. The Calousian Creation Progression accelerates. It does so because we finally understand which knowledge most directly increases our abilities, ourselves, and how we live–i.e., SciTech, science, and the scientific method. Our progression also accelerates because we have an expanding number of institutions and people doing SciTech.

We are now quite near the last stage of Calousian Creation, meaning that we are rapidly increasing our abilities and how we live, and we are about to begin changing our bodies and minds.

In consequence, if we progress as we should–though so far, we're far from it–we could enjoy most of Calousia's astonishing benefits in only about 200 years. In this brief time, we will not complete our full transcendence into Calousians, but we should be able to maximize and virtually maximize, and so complete, the great bulk of the three parts of us. And, remember, the sooner we organize to start this task, the sooner we will enjoy more and more benefits.

You now know that the Advancing Universe progresses through seven quite different stages, each of which produces at its summit the entity or entities necessary for the next advance. Now let's consider what the universe might naturally do after creating Calousians.

Does the AU Continue With a Stage Eight?

Heretofore in this book, I have asked you to think bigger. The subject of this chapter requires you to think far bigger still.

As previously noted, after the Big Bang, universal mass-energy elaborated itself into galaxies, stars, and planets: the theater for the next act. Then, under the favorable conditions that existed on our planet, atoms and molecules aggregated to create life. The biological evolution this initiated progressed until it produced us abilities expanders, beings who can participate in Calousian Creation. We abilities expanders have been playing our appropriate technology-expanding part in Calousian

Creation and have worked our way ever faster toward Calousia.

At Calousia, evolving, progressing mass-energy will have produced two of its highest creations at their most advanced local state; namely, the Calousian individual and Calousia itself. (As noted in Chapter 11, Calousia is a system, consisting of Calousian individuals, their society, their territory, and all the material entities associated with them.)

Once Calousias exist, what happens next? How does the progressing universe continue its advance? Because of the Calousians' high intelligence, extraordinary abilities, and their mastery of SciTech, one would expect great things from these extremely capable beings. Do they cause the universe to keep evolving, but now in some new way? How much further could the progressing universe possibly go?

We can imagine that new Calousias will progressively **expand their individual territories.** They could make their territories bigger by expanding in their part of their galaxy and, perhaps, speed limits permitting, by growing to occupy their entire galaxy and perhaps neighboring galaxies. They could produce this growth by establishing smaller, subsidiary Calousias throughout their territory, the equivalent to towns and cities within a nation. In addition, the Calousian territories in time could become more complex, more organized, and more unified.

We can also imagine a **further expansion**. Calousias, either alone or by working with distant Calousian partners, might vastly expand the number of Calousias in their part of the universe. To accomplish this, Calousias could send settlers farther out into the local universe to establish new

Calousias there, or Calousian agents could help distant pre-Calousians, if they exist, to more rapidly advance.

It's just barely conceivable that this expansion of Calousias **could spread throughout the universe**, like a good virus, so that the entire universe would become speckled with Calousias.

But all these changes, rather than creating something really new, just seem only to multiply the condition of older Calousias. They don't lead to another, quite different kind of progressive universal advance, an advance comparable to those that transformed chemicals into bacteria or bacteria into humans.

What new kind of progressive process would be possible? Calousians can already perform (or soon learn to perform) almost any possible manipulation of biological or inanimate matter. Increasing intelligence can't alter mass energy significantly more. For example, if you synthesize a mega-structure of the mass of a certain moon as fast and efficiently as possible, additional knowledge with respect to this particular synthesis is no help. And as for the elemental forces that appear to govern the future of the universe, we might be able to keep local atoms from disintegrating if that is their natural fate. But considering the colossal size of the massive gravitational and anti-gravitational forces shaping the future of the universe, it's difficult to imagine Calousians doing more than perhaps altering these forces locally.

In short, there seems to be no new progressive universal process that would produce a new or higher universal summit.

It may be, then, that the universe does not progress any further than to Calousias. In this case, the universe may be likened to an annual plant. The plant spouts, grows, flowers, seeds, and dies, in a cycle that repeats itself endlessly. If so, as an old universe begins to wither and die from accelerating expansion, its Calousian seeds, the summit products of universal evolution, could, by compressing small bits of matter, create entirely new universes just as our universe was created from a small mass. Each of these new universes could then evolve to produce new galaxies, stars, planets, life, technology-expanders, and Calousians in a cycle that could repeat itself endlessly, assuming the universe's expanding space has energy, room, and time for these newly created entities.

In consequence, if there is one state in the knowledge-expanding, Calousian-Creating Progression that is so distinctive, knowledge-filled, and capable as to constitute the Summit of the progressive evolution of the universe, Calousia seems to be that condition.

In sum, we've examined a number of changes Calousians might make after becoming Calousian, and none of them seem to offer a new and higher kind of progressive process.

In this case, there would be no universal Stage Eight. It's therefore reasonable to conclude that Calousias are the summit state of the progressive evolution of the universe.

But, **perhaps this reasoning is flawed**, and the universe can and does evolve through a more advanced eighth progressive process that contains its own higher Summit. After all, we are positioned like dinosaurs trying to understand not only the Summit of biological evolution, but how the more advanced creatures at the Summit are likely to progress.

Furthermore, it does seem somewhat wasteful for even our profligate universe, as if it had mind and will, to create these extraordinarily able and knowledgeable Calousians and then have them do nothing crucial to help the progressing universe continue its long advance.

This is especially true when you consider that our earthly Calousians will have so mastered their biological condition as to have set effective maximums to the size of their earthly population. Also, they will have mastered their effective long-term care of their earthly environment. In addition, they will have found the maximums in chemistry, biology, astronomy, energy, engines, transportation, and communication. And, finally, they will have effectively mastered their own self-transcendence into Calousians.

In other words, earthly Calousians would be unusually well positioned to manage the much larger forms and systems of the AU's Stage Eight.

And something else. Up through the AU's Stage Six, the universe advanced through mindless procedures. For example, stars did what their natural conditions and neighboring conditions caused them to do. Atoms and molecules interacted as the characters of their components and local conditions caused them to. In the AU's Stage Seven, our human bodies, minds, and knowledge were promising, but had not advanced enough. But perhaps at Stage Eight, the AU, for the first time in its long progression, needs intelligent, competent management to successfully continue its advance.

Furthermore, just because we cannot yet identify the AU's Stage Eight's progressing formula or how its progressing formula ends, this is an insufficient argument against Stage Eight's existence. Stage Eight is a new concept and once knowledge of it becomes well known, many scientists will come forward with a clearer picture of these Stage Eight aspects. That is some reason to think that the Stage Eight exists and continues the AU's long trajectory.

Finally, it seems egocentric to suppose that the whole purpose of the Advancing Universe is to produce Calousians, superior humans.

Let's then presume that Calousia is not the Summit of the Advancing Universe, that Stage Eight does exist, and that the AU needs the management that Calousians can give it. After all, this is probably true, and it's better for our species to be aware of Stage Eight's existence and to be planning for it, than to be shockingly surprised and unprepared when the Advancing Universe does not end at Calousia.

Do our future high-ability Calousian descendants truly have the awesome responsibility for advancing the AU further? And if so, wouldn't this high-worth, universal task be exciting, challenging, and most interesting?

Such questions about a possible Stage Eight are most important and must be asked and, assuredly, answered. But this subject is beyond the scope of this book.

Of course, whether or not universal conditions provide an eighth progressive process makes no difference to us Stage Seven creatures. We humans should still strive mightily for Calousia because this Summit of Calousian Creation is our species' best possible future.

But can we see Calousia clearly now? Unfortunately, no.

But shouldn't we make sure that we see now the details of the Calousian Summit, a task that will obviously require such unusually great industry and management from us? Shouldn't we clearly see our Calousian-Summit goal before attempting that enormous effort to reach it?

The next chapter explores this reasonable question.

25

WHY WE CAN'T SEE CALOUSIA CLEARLY NOW AND WHY IT DOESN'T MATTER

What will we, as Calousians, look like? How big is our territory? What are our maximized fundamental abilities? How will we live? Do we remain mammal animals? How many eyes do we have? What are our brains like?

Long ago, to understand where accelerating change tended to take our species, I thought that if I could find all the maximums and virtual maximums to our Seven Fundamental Abilities, our bodies and minds, and how we live at the Summit, and all the other significant maximized and virtually maximized aspects of the future, this knowledge should allow me to quite clearly foresee Calousia and Calousians.

Unfortunately, this idea turned out not to be true. Yes, my method could unquestionably prove that a particular aspect of a fundamental ability was limited and therefore the ability maximizable. For example, I am sure that growing technology will not allow us to keep traveling faster, say, between a certain launching place in Chicago and a certain landing one in London. In other words, we can be certain that there is a maximum travel speed over this distance, under the best circumstances, that further SciTech growth cannot exceed.

But even after omitting such facts as the number of people traveling and their baggage, I can't now identify the exact speed maximum over this distance. I don't know where the maximum fits on the span of time slower than the speed of light. And again, considering our incomplete knowledge, it seems unimaginable that the maximum is faster than light speed. But I can't be positive about that, either. In consequence, all these different maximum possibilities, together with no certainty yet as to the correct ones, left my view of the three parts of us disturbingly cloudy.

Fortunately, however, as our knowledge grows, our picture of all three parts of Calousia should become increasingly clearer.

The most important point to understand here, of course, is that **it is not necessary to see Calousia clearly now to be sure that this potential future exists.** We know Calousia exists as a consequence of the distinctive maximized or virtually maximized three parts of us that are fundamental to our self-transformation into Calousians. Just as we know there must be a maximum possible speed in space, we know that Calousia exists. It's like being certain that a particular person must die, but still have little idea of exactly when this death will happen.

It's the fact that Calousia exists that is so powerful when we become aware of it. As you have seen, this knowledge of Calousia's existence changes our view of our species; it changes our relationship with the Advancing Universe; it gives us a primary purpose; and will cause us to undertake this exciting, entirely new activity. We have enough specifics now to take strong pro-Calousian action.

Summary

This chapter explained why, even after proving maximums and virtual maximums of the three parts of us, I was still unable to specifically describe these parts of us at the Calousian Summit.

But it doesn't matter. It's the certain proof that Calousia exists that's important. Meanwhile, our picture of Calousia will get ever more complete and compelling as we advance.

The existence of the Calousian Summit has revealed revolutionary new facts about the universe, about our species, about nations and races. Is it therefore possible that it says new and interesting things about you and me? The next chapter will further explore this question.

26

WHAT THE EXISTENCE OF CALOUSIA SAYS ABOUT YOU AND ME

We've been taking here a larger, universal perspective on our species. It's therefore not unreasonable that this new approach would influence our view of what we human individuals are.

So, yes, in a universe of some two trillion galaxies, on a planet with almost eight billion people fumbling their way forward, the existence of Calousia helps clarify the significance of our species.

But what, specifically, does the existence of Calousia tell us about you and me individually? Since reaching Calousia is our species' primary purpose, it's obvious that what is of first importance for our species–its biggest and most important activity–cannot be irrelevant to us individuals.

But how is it relevant? What does the existence of Calousia mean for us as individuals?

We all well know the arc of traditional individual human existence: birth, childhood, education, growing up, maturing, working, marrying, reproducing and creating families, working at higher levels, and then, toward the end of this arc, for those lucky enough to reach it, retirement, and then death.

On the large scale we've been considering, what do all these individual activities amount to? What do they mean?

Looking at the Past

To find guidance, let's look to the past.

What, for example, did all the activities of all *Homo erectus* individuals mean? What did those of all the individuals of the *Australopithecus* species mean? In our universal perspective, if you exempt a few fossils, all that's left of these previous kinds of individuals and their activities is the role they played in advancing (or delaying) biology's evolutionary progress. In consequence, from the point of view of the progressing universe, specifically its Stage Six, the chief significance of Australopithecus is that this species participated in the creation to Homo erectus, and the chief significance of *Homo erectus* is its part in producing our species.

In other words, in this largest evolutionary perspective, the significance of a species ultimately depends upon the role it plays in the progressive evolution of the universe.

Why, in this AU perspective, should our species be different? Taking this larger perspective on ourselves–on all our individual activities and experiences, however much they dominate our individual time and effort, however profitable, dreadful, destructive, wonderful, joyous, lovable, excruciating, and delightful they may be to us individually–all these activities add up to but one question: Does our species fulfill its self-developing potential and therefore its universal role by reaching Calousia?

In other words, our significance, where we individuals fit in the great scheme of things, depends upon whether our species succeeds or fails to reach the Calousian Summit. This, of course, is because of our species' special position in the AU on account of our being the Summit species of Stage Six and the new material for the AU's Stage Seven.

But note that our significance also depends on something beyond our control. It depends on how many other Ability-Expanders and Calousians exist elsewhere in the universe.

To explain, consider the following **four possibilities:**

Possibility #1: We technology-expanders are just one of many pre-Calousians and Calousians that exist throughout the universe, and we fail.

Here, from the perspective of mass/energy evolving in a two trillion galaxy universe, the significance of our species and of us when we fail must shrivel to virtually nothing. It would be as though neither our species nor any of us individuals had ever existed. The universe must look elsewhere for its advance.

But the consequences for us are even worse than this, because our failure would not be just our own. We would bring to naught all the hard-won advances of all those humans on our planet before us whose efforts had raised us to our present state, and bring to naught as well the great sequence of species that led, directly and indirectly, to our species.

And if in our failing, from a nuclear winter or other disaster, we should destroy not just ourselves but other advanced forms of life on our planet, then slow-advancing biological evolution thereafter might lack the time or the opportunity on our diminished planet to evolve another true abilities-expanding species.

If so, then in failing, we would also be failing all earthly life and, in a sense, failing even Earth itself.

This catastrophe, however, would be local. Elsewhere in the universe, other abilities-expanders and Calousians have or will advance the AU's Stage Seven and perhaps Stage Eight.

Possibility #2: We technology-expanders are just one of many participants in Calousian Creation throughout the universe, and we succeed.

In this situation, the Calousians we create would enjoy the dazzling benefits of Calousian Creation's mature, fully developed state, and we would perhaps join those other Calousians existing elsewhere in the universe as equals and play whatever role that these high-capacity beings, these universal forms, play in the further development of the universe.

Possibility #3: We technology-expanders are the only ones in the universe, and we fail to reach our mature summit state.

In this case, then, from this universal perspective, our individual lives would certainly add up to nothing.

But we would not just be failing ourselves and Earth and our local part of the universe; we would be failing the progressive aspect of the entire universe. It's a thought as awesome as it is pretentious, but who knows? Perhaps it's also true.

Possibility #4: We technology-expanders are the only potential Calousians in the universe, and we succeed.

It's humbling to think that however ambitious we individuals are and however hard we strive to be successful, the role that each of us plays in our scene of the great, progressive, universal drama must be imperceptibly small.

But we individuals are not quite insignificant, for it is our charge and our exciting challenge to create those advanced beings of the future. And this makes all the difference.

If our species is to succeed in transforming itself into those high-capacity Calousians of the future, if these beings will be created in our region of the universe, then we are the ones who must do it.

So if our individual activities help humanity advance, if they help humanity succeed in bringing about its self-transforming evolutionary advance, then even viewing the human progression in the largest perspective, we can be sure our individual lives have influence and are significant. Our lives would impact not only the great arc of human existence but also the progressive advance of the universe itself.

The Calousians we create, being that higher form of intelligent existence and playing that higher role on the universal stage, will enjoy a greater significance than we do. But we also will have a greater significance because we deliberately and successfully created them. Those of us living now won't know the outcome, but at least we will be able to take pride that we have played our appropriate role well.

If we are the only pre-Calousians in the universe–as difficult as this is to believe–and we succeed, then although we are among the tiniest players on the colossal cosmic stage, the advance of universal mass/energy to its evolutionary Summit would now seem to depend utterly upon us. And this is particularly true since we live at that crucial point–between success and failure–in our long

Calousian Creation Progression. Our species would be the means by which the universe continues and, we hope, eventually succeeds in its progressive development. In this strange case, therefore, if our species succeeds, the entire universe succeeds.

Since we are presently aware of no other pre-Calousians or Calousians elsewhere in the universe, **let us accept this larger role for ourselves, as a means to spur us forward**. Let us do this because whatever the case, we know that Calousia is well worth attaining just for its great benefits to ourselves individually and for our species.

Summary

What is the meaning of our individual lives? In the largest perspective, it depends upon (1) what we individuals do, (2) what our species does, and (3) whether other technology-expanders and Calousians exist in the universe.

We don't yet know of any other abilities-expanders or Calousians. We cannot be sure what our species will do. Therefore, let each of us do as much as we can.

Let us rise to the occasion. If we are not quite good enough yet to succeed in the great task before us, let us improve ourselves. Let us make ourselves worthy of the brilliant future that the laws and conditions of the universe offer us. Let us begin now the tasks necessary to succeed in the greatest of all adventures open to us humans. Let us organize and plan our assault now upon that high Calousian peak before us.

You now understand why our Great Progression, our species' greatest achievement, offers us a natural Summit, our species' biggest, richest, best-possible future. You have also explored aspects of this Calousian Summit, including its many astonishing revolutions. And remember that fulfilling our species' astonishing potential depends upon what we do.

So what does all this revolutionary new information prompt us to do next?

This question takes us to Part III of this book: How Do We Reach the Calousian Summit? In Part III we'll consider such questions as: what urgent, momentous choice do we face? What new organizations must we create? And what new revolutions lay ahead of us?

But first, since we humans have been lost, as noted in Chapter 1, we've moved in a number of dangerous, even existence-threatening directions. And since these dangerous directions are a most significant part of our present world, they deserve serious considerations as we plan our advance. Therefore, in the next chapter, the first chapter of Part III, let's briefly review and expand on these existential dangers.

Part III

WHAT MUST WE DO TO REACH THE CALOUSIAN GREATEST-FUTURE SUMMIT?

27

SEVEN DANGEROUS ASPECTS OF THE MODERN WORLD

As we have already noted, **our species faces an existential crisis**. This crisis has many causes. We considered the first four of them in Chapter 1, so I'll note them only briefly here.

Crisis Cause #1: We Are Lost

By calling us lost, to repeat, I mean that, yes, we have long known we were progressing, but we've never known where our progress should take us. This ignorance is costly to our species in time lost, in lives unnecessarily extinguished or wasted in wrong directions. It's costly to us individual humans as well, for we would now live much more advantaged lives if we had awakened to the existence of the Calousian Summit earlier. Finally, it's costly to both our species and us individuals because it has allowed us to move in many difficult-to-correct directions that threaten our extinction.

Crisis Cause #2: Our Human Population Has Exploded

What's so dangerous about our human population explosion? One danger is that our lives are so brief compared to the increase in our numbers that we hardly notice our numbers increasing. This fact dangerously diminishes our perception of the problem and so our urgency in responding to it.

Again, this author, in one long lifetime, was born in 1928 to a world of two billion humans. Now we near eight billion, and by 2050 are expected to reach ten billion, all on a planet of unchanging size.

People today, with our higher standards of living–houses with toilets, hot water, kitchen appliances, TVs, smart-phones, automobiles, etc.–consume far more energy and materials than our ancestors did. We also expect more goods and services–roads, lighting, policing, education, retirement aid, etc.–from our local and national governments.

It's obvious that we cannot, on our fixed-sized planet, continue to have both an increasing human population and all humans enjoying higher living standards. Yes, for a while, we can have ever more people, provided that only a few live in sumptuous luxury and the rest suffer ever decreasing living standards. But do we want this?

If we want all humans to share equally in the benefits of our growing knowledge and abilities, we must set a limit to the number of humans on Earth. And the more we progress, the smaller this number of living humans must be.

Crisis Cause #3: Our Climate Has Degraded

Our increasing population is a major cause of this environmental extinction danger. Our expanding technologies make it worse. The consequence is not just the calamitous mass extinction of other species; it's that our degrading environment is ever less able to support us. We suffer increasingly from pollution, from shortages of arable land and fresh water, and from global warming with its increasing floods, droughts, fires, and ever more destructive storms. This change in our environment unquestionably threatens human existence.

Crisis Cause #4: We Have Created Ever More Destructive Weapons

Humans' long warring tradition has now brought us to the hellish combination of nuclear and biological weapons, inter-continental missiles to deliver them, and artificial intelligence to manage them. The power, number, and availability of these human weapons have grown so great that, for the first time in human history, if unleashed, they could kill us all.

In 1945, the Second World War ended abruptly when just two new fission nuclear weapons incinerated the two Japanese cities of Hiroshima and Nagasaki. Now fusion hydrogen weapons are one thousand times more powerful than either of the two nuclear weapons dropped on Japan.

These four dangers seriously threaten human existence, but there are other dangers we should mention as well.

Crisis Cause #5: The Big Squeeze

Advances in communication and transportation continue, in effect, to drastically shrink our planet as they squeeze us toward a global society. On the whole, this is a good thing. However, squeezing together many different people with their different cherished values and ideas tends to cause tension and conflict.

Furthermore, in our new-forming global society, local time-tested ideas, cultures, and values often no longer work so well. For example, many individuals in the developing world no longer feel satisfied with their lives. They want what those in the advanced world have. In contrast, many many in the advanced world long to return to the simpler conditions of the past.

In addition, as our differentiated world gets increasingly squeezed into one world, problems arising in one nation–disease, crime, drought–tend to spread to other nations.

Crisis Cause #6: Fragmented World, Fragmented Governance

Another dangerous aspect of our modern world is that our world population and governance remain fragmented. Some two hundred countries exist in different environments, whose members belong to different cultures, religions, and races and hold different ideologies and aspire to different goals.

The problem with this fragmentation is less-effective governance among the countries of the world. Nations find it difficult to coordinate to solve common problems. The United Nations unquestionably helps, but any one of the five major nations can stop any proposed UN program. The European Union got off to a good start in governance consolidation, but then the United Kingdom left and other countries may follow. We saw 195 nations sign the Paris Climate Agreement, then the United States left. (Fortunately, the U.S. has returned.) China is trying to expand its territory to reclaim its former high status in the world. Russia is also trying to regain its former territory. But all of us inescapably live in one world now, and this fragmentation keeps us disorganized and backward.

Furthermore, our governance remains organized primarily for a static world, not the dynamic world we increasingly live in, not for our primary progressing, pro-Calousian environment. Also, governance today is reactive; it doesn't look far ahead; its interests don't extend much beyond tomorrow; and its almost 200 entities remain jealous of their independence and protective of their advantages. Look, for example, at the purpose of the United Nations: "Maintaining worldwide peace and security. Developing relations among nations. Fostering **cooperation** between nations in order to solve economic, social, cultural, or humanitarian international problems. Providing a **forum** for bringing countries together to meet the UN's purposes and goals." Yes, this institution certainly helps humanity in many ways, but it's clearly focused on a static world, one requiring only helpful adjustments here and there.

In sum, the primary environment of our species, beginning now and growing more obvious in the future, is our increasingly complex and accelerating progression. This is the new environment we must adjust to in order to be a successful species or even to long exist. Our fragmented world and fragmented governance, being dangerously out of sync with our new primary environment, is very much a continuing threat.

Crisis Cause #7: Problems from Our Increasing Abilities

Our growing SciTech has been giving individuals, organizations, and nations ever-greater abilities. It's an exciting time, for more good things can be done. But, because we were lost–had no idea of where our progress should take us–many of our increasing abilities are **turning dangerous**.

They can give many groups with their different and often conflicting objectives an increasing ability to cause disruption, violence, and chaos. In consequence, bombs, burnings, and killings seem commonplace. Wars these days are not so much between nations as they are between nations and armed groups within them or neighboring them.

Individuals in these groups need little knowledge to acquire and use modern weapons. Newspapers carry pictures of ill-educated youngsters armed with automatic pistols and rifles. More troubling still, some day a small group of terrorists may well get their hands on a nuclear weapon.

Crisis Cause #8: Problems Arising from Our Entering the Last, Rapidly Accelerating Part of Calousian Creation

The last, dangerous aspect of the modern world to be considered here is our entering the final stages of Calousian Creation. As noted, this period differs from previous Calousian-creation times, because it's **rapidly accelerating and increasingly complex.**

What's causing the acceleration? It's because after many tens of thousands of years, our species has finally identified the Calousian goal. We have finally identified both the kinds of knowledge that most directly increases our abilities (i.e., SciTech) and the right method for attaining that knowledge (i.e., the scientific method). This, together with the increasing number of scientists and technologists and the accumulating wealth that keeps them employed, is why our abilities now grow so rapidly. It is the expression of these increasing numbers of abilities that causes the accelerating change in our human condition.

The speed of our accelerating advance means that we must find adequate solutions to an increasing number of complexly interrelated problems in ever less time. It's a recipe for chaos and anger that tends to lead, eventually, to self-destructive conflict.

And think again of that car with no one at the wheel, now speeding at 92 miles per hour and racing faster each minute–oops! Now 94 miles per hour! We're hurtling toward Calousia. We could enjoy this Summit condition very soon.

But acceleration shrinks time, and the speeding not only increases the chance of bad decisions but also expands their impact and multiplies their cost.

When we accelerated slowly, solving problems or even ignoring them caused little difficulty. But now we will face an increasing number of ever-larger problems, many involving the entire world–global warming, terrorism, problems from failing nations, new diseases, etc.–and each often with its biological, cultural, social, economic, ideological, scientific, and technological complexities.

So we must react to these problems ever faster.

And now our car races at 96 miles per hour down a busy road, still going ever faster–and still there's no one at the steering wheel.

So what is the urgent, momentous choice that we humans face? The next chapter provides an answer.

28

OUR URGENT, MOMENTOUS CHOICE

So where are we now? We have been thinking bigger. We know that Calousia exists. We also know it's a far better place than where we are now, and therefore **this truth gives our species an astonishing new primary purpose**. It's to reach Calousia. It's to self-transcend into the higher management-capable Calousian beings that the AU needs at the start of its Stage Eight.

In consequence, we are, for the first time in human history, nay, for the first time in human existence, no longer lost. We know where our species should go and how we should proceed with our astonishing new purpose.

We also know, from Chapter 23, that because we are entering the last Stage of Calousian Creation, where we move faster in increasingly complex conditions, Calousian Creation becomes our primary environment. We either adjust rationally and well to this progressing environment, or we will fail as a species.

Our urgent and momentous task here, therefore, is not whether or not we should try for Calousia. We obviously should try for it, to get the benefits of that better world ahead. That's unquestionable. Remember, we all work for the same Calousian-Creation Company.

Instead, **our urgent and momentous choice is how we should go about reaching Calousia**. It's whether we should essentially continue progressing as we have been, or whether this task requires, if it is to be successful, an entirely new approach, a revolutionary approach–**the creation of a new, world-wide management.**

In other words, do we just continue forward the way we've been going? Or do we grab the wheel, take charge of Calousian Creation, and go for it? That's our choice before us.

Let's look further at these two approaches.

Choice One: Keep to the Present Course

You may think that it is simpler and more practical to just continue our present way forward. In other words, yes, let's advance toward Calousia, but let's not make any really major changes in how we advance. After all, this approach has worked okay so far.

This choice made particular sense when we were unaware that our primary progressive process had a natural, brilliant Calousian Summit. Being unaware, it was easy to think that we were about as advanced as we could practically be now anyway, and that any markedly different future was many lifetimes away, far too distant for present concerns.

It was easy to believe that we should continue to focus on short-term goals, making small advances. We certainly had no incentive to take control of our progressing process. After all, being unaware of the existence of Calousia, where would we attempt to go? SciTech and other knowledge could keep growing forever. We had no particular future to seek, and no way to measure any progress against a meaningful future.

Yes, it's hard to overemphasize the importance of our becoming aware of our potential brilliant Calousian Summit.

But this same-as-before approach is slow, erratic, and–as noted in the last chapter's dangers–more likely to take us to extinction than to Calousia. And if to extinction, human lives would become meaningless, as though we never existed.

No. As I have suggested earlier, if we want to succeed, we can not continue advancing as we have. Reaching Calousia is by far the biggest task our species has ever faced. And getting there is not our human destiny. We can fail in many ways, for example, by over-expanding our population, destroying our environment's ability to keep supporting us, or waging wars with ever more destructive weapons. Furthermore, if we are going to succeed, as with other major tasks we have faced, it will require a deliberate effort and the creation of a great new management appropriate to the size of the great new task we face.

Choice Two: Create New Management

Why take charge? A primary reason for choosing the more aggressive approach is the size and character of our Calousian-Creation task. Our present world is complex and fast-changing, because SciTech creates an increasing number of new kinds of abilities, tools, and products, and these prompt further changes in the economy, society, culture, SciTech itself, and ourselves. As we look to the future, if we keep growing SciTech, we can expect this speed and complexity to accelerate.

Think, for example, of the accelerating introduction of new products as a consequence of emphasizing SciTech growth. Tiny drones, for example. Those making these items are establishing a new small industry, one that creates new jobs and requires more products–like batteries, cameras, radios, and TV monitors–all of which impact the economy. Since these devices can potentially down commercial aircraft, peer into tenth-story apartments, and carry bombs, this product has social aspects and therefore requires new regulations. Drones will influence the environment as their production requires more raw materials and as they help fight fires, for example, and spot other environmental damage. And now drones are even transforming warfare. Yes, this is a small list about a small new product, but it suggests the interactions and the growing complexity of our time.

If you imagine an increasing number of different kinds of new products accelerating at us ever faster, and the complex ramifications of each, you can understand the inadequacy of our present approach to the future.

Our Great Progression is the greatest achievement, so far, of our species. The world-wide task of managing the rest of our way to Calousia is the biggest, most important, most complicated, fastest-changing, and most difficult task our species has ever undertaken. That is why this task must have appropriate, adequate management.

We've undertaken big tasks in the past. We have some experience with bigness. In 1969, for example, the United States put a man on the moon. This eight year effort required, among many other things, new rockets, new rocket ships, new kinds of suits, a way of landing safely, and a way to successfully return the astronauts home. It cost some $25.4 billion.

Do you think it would have been sufficient for President Kennedy to just proclaim the mission to the moon in 1961, start throwing money at it, and let those interested do whatever they could to achieve it? No. To be successful, this big project had to be carefully and persistently managed.

The same could be said of the enormous effort by the United States and other nations to win the Second World War. In today's dollars the war cost the U.S. over $4 trillion and in 1945, the war's last year, defense spending comprised about 40% of GDP.

If the comparatively simple moon mission and the Second World War required careful, persistent management, imagine how much more essential it is to manage the biggest, most difficult task our species has ever faced. If we want accelerating change to take us to Calousia or to any place better than where we are now, the only way we can get there is to take charge of our complex Calousian-Creation process. We cannot succeed with our present approach.

Another point in favor of the take-charge-management approach to Calousia is this: Getting to Calousia may be the biggest, most exciting and important goal, the universal Summit of Calousian Creation, and our species' best-possible future. But, as we have noted, reaching Calousia isn't humanity's destiny. We can fail. In fact, among all the Ability Expanders in the universe, many if not most of them probably fail because this task is so hard to become aware of and so difficult to accomplish. Yes, none of the AU's previous stages on Earth had management or needed it.

But since our Stage Seven is the first here composed of billions of thinking, decision-making individuals, our AU progression requires able management of ourselves to succeed.

There are **Two Advantages to Choosing Management.** The **first** of the advantages of managing Calousian Creation is that our advance will be **faster and more certain**. This in turn means that we and the people who come after us will be more certain to enjoy those future benefits and better lives and to acquire them sooner. In consequence, many more humans will enjoy these improved conditions.

The **second** advantage concerns our species' larger significance. If we don't change the way we advance and cooperate to succeed in our progression, we are more likely to fail and self-destruct than to reach the Calousian summit. If we fail our species' significance in the two trillion galaxy universe will drop to zero. The universe must look elsewhere for its advance.

If, however, we take charge of and manage Calousian Creation, we are far more likely to succeed in reaching Calousia.

And if we do succeed, it means that our entire species will have succeeded, and therefore that all human individuals will also have succeeded–all of us who ever existed. All of us will have a greater significance, for we will have managed the huge task of creating Calousians. This should give us a deep sense of self-satisfaction. Our significance, furthermore, will be even greater because we will have deliberately helped the progressing universe complete its Stage Seven advance here, and the high descendants of ours will no doubt play a significant part in the august activity of the post-Calousian universe.

So What Shall We Do?

Shall we continue to be near-sighted, continue our traditional behavior, and ultimately fail catastrophically? Or shall we organize ourselves sufficiently to maximize our abilities and ourselves and thereby reach this best-possible future at Calousia? In other words, shall we step up and manage Calousian Creation, or shall we continue letting our helter-skelter progression manage us?

With changes coming at us ever faster and the time for adequate responses ever shorter, we can't keep accelerating mindlessly toward increasing chaos and self-extinction. We can't get to Calousia by following the same procedures we have in the past.

The answer is obvious. To be a successful species, to succeed in our self-developing progression, we need not only to "THINK BIGGER," but we must "ACT BIGGER," too.

We must take charge of and carefully manage Calousian Creation, our species' most important process, so we can succeed in it. This approach offers the best means for making present and future human lives better, and this is true whether it's to reach Calousia or just to assure improving human lives. But most important, this new managerial approach is essential for getting us safely, efficiently, and rapidly to Calousia.

Furthermore, **the benefits** from taking control of our inescapable evolutionary condition are so extraordinarily valuable that knowledge of these benefits should unite us to achieve them. This new planet-wide cooperation also greatly increases the probability that our species will succeed in reaching its Calousian Summit.

Finally, undertaking this big, new, world-wide management, as you will see, is doubly revolutionary. First, it will initiate the most exciting, progressive era in human existence, and second, it will take us to the extraordinary new world of Calousian existence.

Summary

Why we should take this entirely new, revolutionary, big management approach to Calousia? I'll give **four reasons**.

First, because reaching Calousia is the newest, biggest, most complex and complicated, and therefore the most difficult task our species has ever undertaken. Success in such a big task requires appropriately big, planet-wide management.

Second, because of the dangers of the modern world–climate change, ever more powerful weapons, etc.–resulting from moving in wrong directions, and the difficulty in correcting these errors.

Third, because of the **high costs** of Calousian Creation **going wrong**. Remember, we have our own self existence and self transformation to manage.

F**ourth**, because of the **great advantages** of our properly and successfully carrying out both our species' role and our universal role.

This aggressive, take-charge management choice will save our species from suffering increasingly difficult, uncertain, and dangerous lives, and an acceleration toward failure and extinction. Instead, taking charge offers us our best chance of ultimate success in reaching Calousia and of individual humans enjoying ever better lives along the way. Taking charge will promote the larger significance of both our species and of us individuals. It will also help guarantee that the universe can continue its progressive advance here.

It's obvious that we must respond reasonably to our growing abilities. This means we must create a new, large-scale system of management appropriate to the new, large-scale task we face.

In sum, this aggressive, take-charge management is really the only sensible choice for us to make. And, since we are already late starting, and since our car now travels at 120 miles an hour, we must start now. Then, just possibly, this one new goal of fulfilling our species' dazzling potential at Calousia, this one big hugely valuable goal all humans have in common, may save us from the far-less-important conflicting goals of nations.

So let's grab the wheel and head for Calousia. Once we do, we will enter the most exciting, progressive, and advantageous era in human history, a revolutionary change from where we are today.

Yes, we are a lost species no longer. So, when do we start?

Next, two questions: Who is really in charge of our Calousian-Creation progression? And if, for some reason, we think *we* are, are we sufficiently capable? The next chapter will answer these questions.

29

WHO IS IN CHARGE? ARE WE SUFFICIENTLY CAPABLE?

Before deciding irrevocably for the larger, more aggressive, take-charge approach to Calousia, one should consider two most relevant questions: first, who is in charge of getting us safely to Calousia? And, second, if we humans are, do we have what it takes to get there? Let's now examine these two questions.

Who Is in Charge?

We need to be very clear about who is in charge of our reaching Calousia. And as this chapter's name suggests, we are, of course. This is obvious. This distinguishes Calousian Creation from all the earlier advancing universal stages–stellar evolution, chemical evolution, etc.–which lacked management and didn't need it. Why? Because the new materials of the earlier stages were atoms, stars, chemicals, etc., not great numbers of thinking, independent individuals.

But if we don't see this responsibility, and don't accept it, as a species and as individuals, all our great advances and strivings so far will come to nothing. We would just be behaving as though we were still lost. Yes, the size and difficulty of these major new responsibilities may cause concern, but they also offer our species a most exciting, high-worth adventure and, ultimately, the best-possible future.

Okay, so we are in charge. Again, we all work for the Calousian-Creation Company. Yes, we do the work, universal conditions determine the results. But now let's face the other most relevant question. Do we have what it takes to manage our species' advance to the Calousian Summit?

Are We Humans Sufficiently Capable?

When we consider all the problems and conflicts in our fragmented world today and the inability of our governments to solve them, it does not inspire confidence.

Getting to Calousia sounds easy. All we must do is keep growing SciTech and keep adjusting reasonably to the resulting changes in conditions until the three parts of us expand to fill that Calousian mold of limits. But remember that while reaching Calousia may be our most exciting task, it's also the largest, fastest-changing, most complex, and most difficult task our species has ever attempted.

Again, we are already late getting started. Our task would have been easier some fifty years ago. But we kept drifting. We let our advances in SciTech double the world's human population since 1973. Had we not done this, humans today could be better educated, healthier, wealthier, and facing less conflict because of far-less-extreme problems of pollution, global warming, and shortages of water, agricultural land, and energy. In consequence, humans today would be far more advantaged, living better lives, and, undoubtedly, far closer to Calousia.

Meanwhile, changes in our human condition continue to accelerate. Our car now speeds toward 130 miles per hour, going ever faster, ever more out of control, ever closer to catastrophe, and still no one's at the wheel.

We probably have the ability both to take charge of our evolutionary process and to succeed in it. We have much to learn, but the world exhibits some examples of good, forward-looking activity and governance at the local, national, and international levels, and these at least suggest we have the capacity.

But what if this really isn't true?

Well, if we think we lack the ability, then we won't even try, and consequently we will certainly fail. We would never receive all the benefits of our further advance. We would fail even though, in fact, we did have the capacity and could have succeeded.

Therefore, even if, unknown to us, we truly lack the ability, we should still behave as though we have it. It's only by this means that we can make the best of ourselves. It's our best option.

If our species is to fulfill its brilliant potential in Calousian Creation, we need to start now.

Remember what will happen if we don't take control and don't manage our abilities-expanding, Calousian-Creation process–if we don't grab the wheel. We will keep accelerating haphazardly toward certain self-extinction.

But our failure would really be worse than even self-extinction. This brings us to the second surprising claim made in Chapter 19. It has to do with our place in the universe, a universe two trillion times larger than we thought just one lifetime ago. This surprise is that as relatively tiny as Earth is in this colossal universe, and as infinitesimally much smaller than Earth we human individuals are, we humans are nevertheless the most advanced part of the known advancing universe, and we have a most important universal role to play.

If our species cannot fulfill its extraordinary Stage Seven potential, the advancing universe locally must seek its advance to the Calousian Summit elsewhere.

In other words, the second surprise from Chapter 19 is that if we don't take charge of our Calousian-Creation process, we risk failing not only our entire species and all those who have advanced us to our present state but–in a way–we fail the progressing universe itself.

Therefore, to avoid this catastrophe, to fulfill our species' brilliant potential, and to take advantage of all of Calousia's extraordinary benefits, let's head for Calousia.

Summary

In a universe of two trillion galaxies, does our comparatively microscopic species have what it takes to reach Calousia? I think we do.

But even if I'm wrong and we don't have what it takes, it's advantageous for us to organize and keep progressing as though we do have the capacity to succeed. This is because, under these new conditions, we might well be able to succeed.

We've now made the case several times that our Calousian-Creation progression cannot succeed without a whole new level of management. But what, precisely, does this mean? The next chapter will explain.

30

WHAT ARE THE SEVEN NEW, WORLD-WIDE ORGANIZATIONS WHICH WE MUST CREATE?

What does "taking charge" and "a whole new level of management" mean? It means we must not only maximize and virtually maximize the three parts of us and rationally adapt to them – major tasks–but we must also undertake the larger, much more difficult task of organizing and persistently managing ourselves. It means that we must learn how to successfully progress from where we are now–in SciTech, in our natural, social, and man- made environments, and in our pre-Calousian bodies–all the way up to Calousia and becoming Calousians. Then we must adjust rationally to these new maximized or near-maximized three parts of us. Yes, it's our species' biggest and most important task and, fortunately, it's also a very doable task. But to succeed in this task, we need adequate management.

This means management appropriate to the world-wide size, complexity, and rapid change of the task we face. It also means management that's competent, has access to accurate, relevant knowledge, is sufficiently funded, and has been given the necessary authority to take us efficiently, safely, and reasonably soon to the Calousian Summit.

To start this greatest, most important, and revolutionary task, we must create seven new world-wide organizations, institutional components of a larger planet-wide governance.

The first two organizations concern the relationship between our species and our environment.

Organization #1 has the purpose of maintaining and improving our **environment.** We must create this new organization because our environment is precious and because the more we degrade it, the more costly and uncertain our advance. Yes, many environmental organizations already exist, but they are not yet anywhere near as effective as they must be to get us to Calousia.

Organization #2 has the purpose of setting and maintaining the size of our world-wide **human population.** Biological creatures tend to multiply and are kept in check by aspects of their environment. Our growing SciTech has helped us humans avoid the kinds of environmental factors that keep the numbers of other species in check. Larger organisms, like tigers, now seldom eat us, and environmental threats like freezing and intense heat seldom kill us. And even our control over smaller organisms, like bacteria and viruses, improves. So our human population has expanded. I was born in what we then thought was a crowded world of about two billion of us. We now approach eight billion and this increase is a major factor in the increasing degradation of our biosphere.

But, as noted above, we deeply depend on our environment not just for our survival, well-being, and delight, but also for our success in reaching the Calousian Summit. This is because the more our growing population degrades our environment, the more costly, difficult, and improbable our advance becomes.

Therefore, to succeed in our Calousian Creation, we must keep our human population numbers appropriate to our small planet's healthy biosphere. The right number of us as we advance will not be a fixed quantity, but must change with other changes in ourselves, in our environment, and in the specific conditions of our changing progression.

To appropriately manage this changing human population number on our planet, we must establish an Earthly Population Organization. This institution should set, at regular intervals, specific, needed human population decreases and/or increases. It should have access to reliable information necessary for good decisions, and the authority to enforce these decisions.

Controlling our population size is a new concept and it will not be easy. But we must gain control over this biological part of us to keep our environment healthy and supportive during our Calousian-Creation progression. Without such an institution, we will have no chance of fulfilling our species' extraordinary potential.

The next two organizations are concerned with managing our Calousian-Creation Progression.

Organization #3 has the purpose of **planning** how best to reach Calousia. We must create this world-wide research and planning organization and charge it with identifying, in its publications, the best route for reaching the Calousian Summit. For this purpose, the organization should identify important, attainable, and measurable goals which relevant governments and institutions should achieve by specific target dates. These goals and progressions should be regularly and formally reviewed, updated, and published.

The planning organization must obviously be aware of present trends, and must try to determine where various future SciTech growth will create new opportunities and problems, and what influence these will have on the economy, the society, the environment, etc., and how best to adjust from present conditions to these future conditions.

This planning institution should rely on its own studies and those of other institutions–like those in this chapter and elsewhere, including the UN and national and local governments–to carry out their mission of finding the best way of soon reaching the Calousian summit.

Organization #4 has the purpose of **managing** the plan created above for advancing to Calousia. This organization will be the practical facilitator. Its task is to get things done. It's the real manager of our advance to our mature-abilities condition at Calousia. Its task is to work with national governments, international organizations like the UN and its various specialty groups, and all relevant others to help them be aware of, contribute to, and carry out the plans of the other pro-Calousian organizations.

It's better if this management organizes and guides nations and other organizations to right action rather than being dictatorial. But to be effective it needs sufficient authority, some way to reward those doing well and to punish the poor performers. Perhaps this can be accomplished by giving it an independent taxing authority. Giving these wide powers to this new kind of organization will obviously cause new difficulties, but failing to give it adequate powers is equivalent to allowing our species to long delay or fail to fulfill its dazzling potential.

Rewards could include funding and awarding honors and citations to those individuals and groups that have made notable pro-Calousian advances. Also, a "Calousia Day" might be created as a time each year to make awards, celebrate Calousian-advancing achievements, and remind us of essential tasks to accomplish and encourage us to achieve them.

The next two new organizations are tasked with growing the specific knowledge needed to reach the Summit.

Organization #5 has the purpose of **growing** the relevant **SciTech** for our Calousian goal**.** We must create this organization to periodically identify, promote, and help create the primary SciTech needed to advance to Calousia, particularly those advances that lead to the maximizing or virtually maximizing of the two parts of us: namely, our Seven Fundamental Abilities and our bodies and minds. The third part of us will be dealt with below.

Presently, the high cost of new experiments and the shortage of funds often force the creation of groups of scientists–of astronomers, for example–to prioritize among various possible costly tools and experiments. In consequence, much of the needed information for this new organization is already out there. The organization could acquire it from international organizations, like the UN;

from national and state governments; from scientific organizations, published papers, and from contact (personal, e-mail, etc.) with particularly well-informed individual scientists.

Therefore, this task could be accomplished by a relatively small, well-informed staff with wide contacts among scientists around the world, particularly those in scientific organizations–governmental and non-governmental–already charged with targeting new knowledge. But to be successful, this organization will need appropriately large funding.

The radical change from the past here is one of perspective. We must not only think bigger; we must now focus on growing the SciTech that maximizes those three parts of us. Again, the third part of us will be dealt with below. The second part of us follows.

Organization #6 has the purpose of **managing our species' self-transcendence** into Calousians. Up to now, our SciTech has remained too primitive for such a task to make sense. But, as noted in Chapter 10, **three recent technologies** promise to bring this genetic area from the far future toward the present.

The first is **gene sequencing**, which identifies genes, specifically the order of the four basic nucleotides along our chromosomes. Therefore, for the first time in human existence, individuals can learn of defective genes they carry.

The second new technology, already noted, is **CRISPRcas9**. This technology, and improvements in it, will allow individuals to replace defective genes during conception with good ones, and eventually with better ones.

The CRISPR technology has been used to treat congenital blindness, sickle-cell disease, heart disease, nerve disease, cancer and H.I.V. The greatest obstacles are not technical but legal, financial and organizational.

The third recent technology is the **Human Cell Atlas**, which has the goal of identifying and placing all the 37 trillion cells in the human body together with their molecular makeup and function.

So the genie is already out of the bottle. We already rush rapidly toward this unfamiliar new world of a deeper understanding of our human bodies and how to correct and change our genes. Growing SciTech will unquestionably allow us to make increasing genetic changes in our children at conception and in ourselves as well. The only question is: Do we take charge of this process now, and rationally work ourselves toward ever-better lives? Or do we just let individuals–experts and small groups, and corporations make inheritable changes–some helpful and many painfully harmful–and just hope it works out for the best? The answer is obvious. This area is too crucial to leave unmanaged.

Organization #7 has the purpose of promoting **coordination** among the above organizations, to make sure that all advance appropriately and in harmony with each other and with the World Government's other tasks. It is composed of the leaders of the other organizations plus a staff.

Remember, we no longer live in a relatively static world. The primary new environment of our species and of the individual members of our species, too, is our Calousian-Creation progression. It's primary because this is the new environment that we must adjust to if we are going to reach Calousia, have ever-better lives, or long survive. As noted, our increasing abilities make this environment increasingly complex, dynamic, and fast-changing with economic, social, and cultural consequences. To survive in this increasingly complex world, to keep us from going off in poorly thought out, self-defeating directions, we must manage our advance. And now that we are no longer lost, and therefore, for the first time in human existence, know where to go, this management, this planet-wide control of our progressive, evolutionary self-development, this last, new, greatest of all revolutions–set in motion by the creation of the seven new organizations just noted–is essential.

The Odds

What do you think are the odds that we can create the seven new kinds of management organizations with their specialists to determine how best to advance?

Not too bad, perhaps?

And what are the odds that our citizens and political leaders will agree to follow these plans?

Mediocre, you say?

Well, these are also the present odds that ours will be a successful species. This management for succeeding in our species' primary purpose is this big picture that helps put into perspective many of our other problems: educational, environmental, economic, scientific, and our expanding population.

In sum, humanity faces many problems, but none are more important than our beginning to effectively manage our species' biggest, most important endeavor: our Calousian-Creation Progression. If we cannot learn to create and maintain the management of this accelerating and increasingly complex progression, we have no hope of fulfilling our species' astonishing potential.

We've now looked at five amazing revolutions. Can the perception of the existence of Calousia produce still another revolution? We will consider this interesting question in the next chapter.

31

REVOLUTION #6: IMPLEMENTING HUMANITY'S GREAT PROGRESSIVE ERA

I have now explained **five revolutionary changes in perception**, changes that are essential if our species is to be successful. **Revolution #1** is the identification of our long progression's Calousian Summit and therefore knowledge of where our progress should take us; **Revolution #2** is the great change in our perception of our species' relationship with the Advancing Universe; **Revolution #3** is the great change in our perception of what we humans really are; **Revolution #4** is the great change in our perception of our primary environment; and **Revolution #5** is the great changes in our perception of races, cultures, and nations.

However, the next two essential **Revolutions, #6** and **#7**, are different. These revolutions are not just big changes in perception; they are big economic, social, and knowledge-growing revolutions. And here, of course, it's all of you who must do the work of creating and advancing these revolutions.

Revolution #6 really began many tens of thousands of years ago, with the arrival of our modern human species on Earth. This AU Stage Seven really didn't look progressive to us when we entered the Agricultural Revolution and the Urban Revolution. It just seemed that some people preferred to live one way and others another way. But our human existence certainly began looking progressive as we entered the Industrial Revolution and our modern period, the latter often called the Communication Revolution. Nevertheless, our progress remained erratic and slow.

The part of Calousian Creation that I want to consider here, as briefly noted in Chapter 16, is the part I call **Revolution #6**: the Calousian-Creation Revolution. It begins when we first start organizing to reach Calousia and ends at Calousia itself. This part of Calousian Creation should be far more revolutionary than any other of our Stage Seven parts.

Why? Because it's the only period of our long, Calousian-Creation Progression in which our advance will be deliberate, organized, and managed. Therefore, instead of being disorganized, slow, and haphazard as our Stage Seven has been heretofore, we can expect this new period to be extremely rapid and fast changing.

This sixth revolution will produce **the most exciting, dynamic, and progressive era in human existence**. Members of our species will rapidly grow SciTech and other essential knowledge. This will produce great economic changes that result from all the new products and services, and significant social change on a world-wide scale as we organize ourselves and create the essential management structures.

We will adjust to these new realities with the growth of not just more knowledge, but also with a continuing expansion of our human abilities and the fast improvements in both our bodies and minds and in how we live.

This exciting, dynamic, and progressive era will end at the Calousian Summit as we maximize or virtually maximize these three parts of us and complete the revolutionary creation of Calousia and Calousians.

In other words, this last part of Calousian Creation will be revolutionary in its purposefulness, coordination, and rapid and certain progress; in the great number, size, complexity, and significance of its advances; and in its supreme achievement of reaching the Calousian Summit.

In consequence, these revolutionary changes in our perception of our species, of our place in the AU, of our species' purpose and how to achieve it, will produce **a revolutionary new era** in human existence. These great changes will divide our long Calousian-Creation Progression into two quite different parts: the earlier, traditional, unaware-of-the-Summit, and unmanaged part and the later aware, organized, and managed part.

The early part was slow-advancing, unorganized, erratic, and focused on lesser activities, such as life-or-death competitions between city states or between nations, all temporary entities. This earlier part also had us disposed to avoidable crises, such as overpopulation, climate change, and wars with ever more destructive weapons. In sum, it's most improbable that this earlier approach can take us to Calousia.

In contrast, the later part of our progression will be purposeful, managed, dynamic, exciting, fast-progressing, and with a very good chance of reaching the Calousian Summit.

What should we call this latest, most revolutionary period of our long Calousian-creation advance? I suggest we call it the **"Race to the Summit."**

Is this Race to the Summit a **universal** phenomenon? Of course, we don't know. But elsewhere, too, in the early days, Calousian Creation would probably start slowly, progress little, so ability-expanders would have no reason to think they were in a progression. And later, even when they realize they do participate in a progression, they, too, would likely be slow to understand where their advances should take them, and therefore also be slow to organize their approach to their progression. And, finally, once they realize that the advantageous Calousian Summit exists, they would start organizing themselves to reach this Summit and reach it as soon as possible, so they, too, would experience the "Race to the Summit."

By this argument, the above sequence of events, the "Race to the Summit" is probably typical of Calousian Creation universally, but with lots of variations.

As I've shown, our Calousia-Creating Progression is not just a local condition. It's also the AU's Stage Seven here, including its natural, universal Summit.

We've now looked at six revolutions resulting from the existence of the Calousian Summit. Might there also be a seventh revolution? The next chapter will explore this question.

32

REVOLUTION #7: THE POST-CALOUSIAN PROGRESSION

Yes, reaching Calousia marks the end of our Stage Seven Calousian-Creation progression. But now it seems unlikely to be the end of the AU's progression. After all, as noted, it seems to make no sense–as if the universe could think–for the AU to create Calousians, beings with abilities, bodies and minds, and ways of living far above us humans, beings who can manage their population size, their planetary environment, and their successful advance to the Stage Seven Summit, and then make no use of these advanced beings to progress still further.

That's why the Calousian Summit probably just marks the beginning of another kind of universal progression, one on a much higher level–the AU's Stage Eight or the post-Calousian Progression.

Assuming this assumption is correct, the next essential revolution, **Revolution #7,** would begin with our arrival at Calousia: the beginning of the AU's Stage Eight.

What will this new Stage Eight be like? How will it end? Of course, we don't yet know.

Nevertheless, as we near Calousia, we should try to gain some insight into this next, more advanced kind of universal progression.

You may think this consideration of the AU's Stage Eight as unrealistically premature. After all, we still have so much to learn about the Stage Seven Summit, and we are not even sure that a Stage Eight exists.

Yes, it does seem unrealistic at first. But I mention our potential Stage Eight here because **we don't want to repeat the bad start** we made with Stage Seven. Back then, and for a long time, we didn't even realize we were in a progression, and, after that, we didn't understand that we were in charge of our progression until we neared the end of it. So we were lucky to understand these Stage Seven realities before it was too late.

In consequence, as we near Calousia, we should already be thinking about what comes next. That way we will be more prepared for the very new post-Calousian conditions, more ready to adjust to these new situations, and, consequently, more likely to succeed in them, all providing, of course, that this Stage Eight exists.

The task we face now, therefore, is **why would this post-Calousian Summit world be revolutionary**? One reason is because it's likely to be profoundly different from our Stage Seven, with its concentration on us ability expanders growing the three parts of us to the maximum or virtual maximums. Also, Stage Eight promises to give us one of two quite different kinds of "universes."

The **first** of these new Stage Eight universes may be like that annual plant, noted earlier, the one that grows, flowers, seeds, withers, and then dies. In this case, after reaching its Stage Seven Calousian Summit, the new AU "world" might be the unattractive one of withering and dying. Matter and even space may start disintegrating. Instead of the optimism of the Calousian-Creation period, this would present an ever increasingly difficult period. This is certainly a revolutionary change, but not one we'd look forward to. However, it may be one in which our high capabilities and management skills could prove to be of crucial service.

The **second** kind of revolutionary "world" change is perhaps more probable and certainly far more desirable. It's that the AU will use us just-produced and superbly knowledgeable and capable Calousians to continue its advance in an entirely new way that only these advanced beings can make possible and succeed in.

This new "world" will be revolutionary also in the sense that heretofore we had concentrated, so to speak, on preparations for our great Calousian feast, i.e., on reaching Calousia. Now we can enjoy eating it, i.e., take pleasure in our Calousian existence, while also preparing for the further new adventures of the AU's Stage Eight. The transformation in this new Stage Eight would be comparable to, but much higher than, Stage Five's chemicals complexing into living bacteria, or Stage Six's bacteria transcending into us humans.

As we attempt to foresee the AU's Stage Eight, as with the AU's earlier stages, we must identify its two starting conditions and the two ending ones. We already know one of the starting conditions. It's us Calousians. We will be Stage Eight's new material. Unfortunately, we don't yet know Stage Eight's new progressive formula or its two ending conditions.

It's likely, however, that the universal Calousian beings we create will find themselves involved in a new and even bigger universal process. Since Calousians cannot much improve themselves, perhaps they can improve the way the universe progresses. For example, they might stop it from going in dangerous, less-advanced directions, and nudge it into a much newer and better, more advantageous direction. Whatever this higher AU way of progressing is, we can be sure that it will be quite different, most exciting, and a brand new, major-revolutionary adventure with fabulous advances.

Yes, the odds are good that we will face a huge, new, vastly different Seventh Revolution, one that we future Calousians can look forward to.

You have seen this book's title many times. But let's now put it in a chart and consider it a little more carefully.

Why "Thinking Bigger" is our Essential Guide to Humanity's Greatest Future

1. Before the essential Thinking Bigger guide, we humans were **lost.** We knew we were in a Great Progression, but it wasn't that important to us. And by degrading our environment and waging ever more horrific wars, we drifted toward an **early self-extinction.** (See pages 2-11, 220-227)

2. Thinking Bigger provides essential guidance by identifying, for the first time, **Humanity's Greatest Future** – our Great Progression's natural Calousian Summit. (See pages 1-131)

3. This new "greatest-future" gives our whole species, again for the first time, the new **primary purpose** of striving for this superior summit future. It's the best goal for both our species and the Advancing Universe. (See pages 168-178)

4. Finally, Thinking Bigger guides by detailing, for the first time, the revolutionary, new, **means** for reaching our greatest future. (See pages 220-251)

Yes, these are the reasons Thinking Bigger is "the essential guide to humanity's greatest future."

So if our self-developing species is to fulfill its greatest potential, if human lives are to get ever bigger, richer, and better, and greatest of all at the Calousian Summit, then "Thinking Bigger" truly is our species "Essential Guide to Humanity's Greatest Future." And, most hopefully, as you will see, your essential guide as well.

So now, let's return to our Stage Seven situation. Is there anything that you, the individual, can do to help our advance to Calousia? The next chapter will answer these questions.

33

HOW YOU MIGHT HELP: ACCEPT RESPONSIBILITY AND ACT ACCORDINGLY

Why is it essential to include in this book possible pro-Calousian tasks that you, the reader, might undertake?

The answer is because reaching **the Calousian Summit must be a highly cooperative social task.** Therefore, if a preponderance of you readers, who now understand the task, don't effectively make a pro-Calousian effort, then our species will continue being lost, and our descendants will never experience the brilliance of the Calousian Summit.

Our human species has the primary purpose of fulfilling its extraordinary potential by reaching Calousia. It therefore stands to reason that each member of our species who is aware of Calousia's existence has an inherent responsibility to help reach that brilliant goal. If too few of us accept this new role, then our species must just ultimately fail both itself and the Advancing Universe.

On the other hand, the more each of us helps, the more likely our ultimate success and the more our lives are in harmony with our progressing species and the progressing universe. And this is true whether our species ultimately succeeds or fails to reach Calousia.

And, again, even if our goal were not to reach Calousia, but just to work our way toward a future of better, more advantaged lives for every human individual, it would be essential to start managing our advance in that Calousian direction now. We would still need to take charge now.

Yes, humanity faces many problems, but none is more important than effectively managing our species' success in its biggest, most important activity. And now, when such management has not yet even been attempted, there is no better opportunity for the individual to make a difference. I urge you, the reader, to do all you can to help our species fulfill its brilliant potential.

There is satisfaction in knowing that you participate not just in a high purpose, but in humanity's most important purpose. And, of course, you are also helping the progressing universe succeed in reaching its Stage Seven Summit. In addition, there is the personal challenge, and the potential satisfaction of making a notable contribution toward that advance, the highest cause of the one species we all have in common.

Yes, you and I won't enjoy all those future advantages, but we and our children will enjoy the increasing benefits.

The good life means different things to different people. But if you think that at least one element of the good life is to put oneself in harmony with both the progressive direction of our species and that of the universe, here are four obviously important areas where you might choose to help in our advance now–alone or with others.

1. Help spread word of the existence of Calousia and why we should strive for this Summit.

For example, find ten people unaware of the Calousian Summit, then inform them about both this Summit and its astonishing benefits. And then urge each of these ten people to do the same with ten more individuals.

2. Help create our Calousian-Creation Management-to-the-Summit Organization.

As noted, our long Calousian-Creating Progression is our species' biggest and most important activity. We have now identified, for the first time, the natural, brilliant Summit of this progression. We have learned where our long progression should take us. We know of the crises resulting when this increasingly fast and complex process remains unmanaged. It therefore makes sense, for the first time, to create an appropriate, new, world-wide management for this progression, so we can reach this Summit more certainly and sooner. This task is obviously very difficult, because it's big (world-wide) and because such management of such a new, long-term purpose has never existed before. But we've already created large-scope organizations. Examples include: the United Nations, the EU, the world-wide organizations to control the Covid pandemic, the multi-national organizations associated with the UN and those separate from it to manage particular large problems. But considering the dangers we face–e.g., environmental degradation and nuclear weapons–and the increasing speed and complexities ahead, this new management is also the best way to avoid our species' early self-extinction. But if we are going to be a successful species, fulfill our extraordinary potential, play our species' most important role for itself and for the AU's Stages Six, Seven, and even Eight, or even long survive, we must create this new, world-wide management of our increasingly complex and fast-changing Calousian-Creating Progression.

We already participate in our Great Progression, our species' biggest achievement. The purpose of this new management is to help us succeed in our progression, to make human lives ever better and reach our progression's natural Summit more certainly and sooner. This management is essential if our species is to attain its best future and fulfill its extraordinary potential. That's why you should get involved here.

Changes here are not easy, but they are essential. So if you can, try to advance this world-wide governance. If that is not possible, help improve and/or expand these needed governance areas locally.

3. Get involved in other specific aspects of our Calousian Creation progression.

For example, help promote the growth of SciTech (i.e., STEMM knowledge) particularly among the Seven Fundamental Abilities, (Chapter 9), or of our bodies and minds (Chapter 10), or of improvements in how we live with our growing knowledge. Again, many organizations already exist in these areas. But a bigger, better, long-term, purposeful, and overall management organization is what's eventually needed. And, of course, better education is needed everywhere.

4. Join us at the Calousian Association

www.calousia.world
PO Box 607, Mill Valley, CA 94942.

This tax-exempt organization promotes awareness that our species' Great Progression has a natural Summit and the great advantages of reaching this Summit. This organization also works in many ways to help our species succeed in attaining this vastly superior future.

Yes, please, please do as much as you can to help our lost, threatened species gain new control over our Calousian-Creation Progression so we can succeed for our species and for the Advancing Universe.

Evaluation

The brilliant and astonishing summit-world of Calousia awaits us. But our car now hurles us forward at 140 miles per hour, and that last bump even took us airborne for two or three seconds. And, still, no one's at the wheel.

Reaching Calousia will be difficult because it requires us to change our ways–altering, for example, some of our attitudes, behaviors, and cultural norms–and people tend to strongly resist such changes.

Does this task I have presented sound impossibly difficult?

If so, then it's appropriate to repeat two earlier questions: What are the odds that we can create the necessary plans for our advance-to-the-Summit organizations? What are the odds that our political leaders will agree to follow these plans?

Do you still find these odds low?

If so, then these are the current odds against our species being successful.

But isn't our species better than this? Must we allow our unmanaged, haphazard, and fragmented Calousian-Creation Progression to end sooner than we expect in a meaningless extinction, one that obliterates not only all our species' marvelous advances but those of almost all other earthly life, as well?

Can't we think and act bigger and wiser than we have before? Can't we also be realistic about our human condition and make the most of it, and thereby truly fulfill our species' most remarkable potential?

Yes, we can. Because we are now appropriately thinking bigger. We can harness our new perceptions of ourselves and of our potential future to power our species' astonishing new purpose. We can then follow this essential guide and thereby succeed in fully completing our species' most extraordinary self development. And, yes, we can begin to take charge of our grand Calousian-Creation process now

(Good luck, you most promising species).

You have now finished "Thinking Bigger." Good for you! And think of all the very different ways that this book has encouraged you into thinking bigger. To quickly help with this, I've added one last chart, as follows:

Examples of Thinking Bigger

1. About what we humans really are:

Before experiencing Thinking Bigger (TB) we considered ourselves, like other species, in static terms: e.g., sapiens, tool user, and culture bearer.

After TB, we see ourselves as dynamic self-developing, self-transforming, and self-transcending beings, the creators of Calousians, and playing roles in the Advancing Universe's Stages 6, 7, and 8.

2. About how universal processes created us:

Before TB: we focused on biological processes that created us.

After TB: we see how the Advancing Universe (AU) created us in a series of very different stages, the first going all the way back to the Big Bang.

3. About our Great Progression:

Before TB: We knew we had been progressing, but were unsure where it should take us. We were lost, wandering in dangerous directions, such as climate change and unnecessary wars with ever more horrific weapons.

After TB: now knowing of the Summit's existence, reaching it assumes primary importance, and the progression itself increasingly becomes our primary environment.

4. About our human role in the Advancing Universe (AU):

Before TB: any human role in the universe seemed preposterous.

After TB: great new human roles revealed in the AU's 6th, 7th and 8th stages.

5. About our species' appropriate role:

Before TB: our species' social roles were essentially local, national, and slowly growing toward global.

After TB: we see all humanity's role as being totally responsible for completing our species' self-development into Calousians.

6. About how best to reach the Calousian summit:

Before TB: we continued our slow, haphazard disorganized approach.

After TB: we realize that our approach must be organized and persistently managed on a global scale to the Calousian summit.

7. About our individual roles toward the Calousian Summit:

Before TB: none, no Summit existed.

After TB: we individuals realize that helping humanity reach the Calousian Summit is our most important activity.

8. About the Post-Calousian revolution:

Before TB: no thoughts ever about this particular revolution.

After TB: to really understand what we are, and properly play the roles the AU give us, we must start thinking about this larger future condition now.

BIBLIOGRAPHY

Brondizio, E, et al., *Intergovernmental Science-Policy Platform on Bio- diversity and Ecosystem Services: IPBES,* Global assessment report on bio- diversity and ecosystem services of the Intergovernmental Science-Policy Platform on Biodiversity and Ecosystem Services, https://www.unep.org/annualreport/2022/.

Bush, Vannevar. *Science - The Endless Frontier.* A Report to the President. Office of Scientific Research and Development. July 1945.

Everrett, Daniel. *Don't Sleep, There are Snakes and Language in the Amazonian Jungle,* Pantheon Books. 2008.

Greenhalgh Albion, Robert, and Phelps Hall, Walter. *A History of England and the British Empire*. 3rd Edition. Gina and Co. 1946.

Kuzma, Samantha, et al., *25 Countries, Housing One-quarter of the Population, Face Extremely High Water Stress,* https:// www.wri.org/insights/ highest-water-stressed-countries. 2023.

Lee, H, and Romero, J (eds.). *Climate Change 2023: Synthesis Report*. Contribution of Working Groups I, II and III to the *Sixth Assessment Report of the Intergovernmental Panel on Climate Change (IPCC)*, Geneva, Switzerland, doi: 10.59327/IPCC/ AR6-9789291691647.

Regev, A., et al., *The Human Cell Atlas*. Elife. Dec 5;6. pii: e27041. doi: 10.7554/eLife.27041.

Saayman, Sheena, et al., *The therapeutic application of CRISPR/ Cas9 technologies for HIV*, Expert Opinion on Biological Therapy, 15:6, 819-830, DOI: 10.1517/14712598.2015.1036736, 2015.

Sender R, Fuchs S, Milo R. (2016), *Revised Estimates for the Number of Human and Bacteria Cells in the Body*. PLoS Biol 14(8): e1002533. https://doi.org/ 10.1371/journal.pbio.1002533.

Index

About the Author

Warren Musser grew up in the fast-changing San Francisco Bay Area of California. During World War Two, while he was in High School, the population of his town, Alameda, tripled. He then moved with his mother and her new husband to the East Coast during which time he enlisted in the U.S. Army and graduated from Yale (a BA in literature, history, and psychology). He also inherited some money, not enough to live on, but if he lived simply, it provided some freedom and security. Due to his good education, health and money, Musser felt a duty to contribute in some way.

Since he could compose small pieces while at the piano, he thought it reasonable to expand this ability. So he spent three years at Juilliard studying symphonic composition. He failed. He didn't progress fast enough. Although he was sure he could eventually write symphonies, he didn't know if they would ever be good enough to warrant the great effort.

Dejected, he returned to the Bay Area. He found it had continued changing during his 14 years away–populated now with a million more people.

These increasing Bay Area changes enormously impressed him. Where, he wondered, did these changes tend to take not just Californians, but all humanity? Of course, virtually everyone knew our species had begun as hunters and gatherers, and that we had made extraordinary progress since then. And a number of authors had expressed near-term future views. But no one knew more than that. Musser realized that our species was lost, we had no idea where our progress should take us.

Moreover, being lost is dangerous. It has us going off in wrong directions, like climate change, environmental deterioration, our population surges, excessive nationalism, and wars with ever more destructive weapons. In addition, if we knew where our progress should take us, we could begin deliberately striving to get there, and we would be far more certain of getting there. Musser thought that perhaps this was an area where he could contribute.

So in the evening of October 1, 1960 in spite of his inadequate background in this multi-disciplinary area, Musser decided to devote his life to trying to find out where our long progression should best take us. Thus began years of intensive reading in the sciences, technology, and other relevant areas.

But could Musser succeed in such a multi-disciplinary task way beyond his formal education? A suggestion of the answer came a few years into his human future project, because Musser ran into a problem. He and his new wife, Elizabeth Quam, a cellist, needed a home in Mill Valley, a small town north of the Golden Gate Bridge. Musser couldn't afford to buy a house, rents were high, and, of course, the greater his housing costs, the more he must work to earn money, and the less time and energy he would have for his future studies. So Musser decided to build his house himself.

His most relevant previous experience here was making a wooden wastepaper basket in grammar school. Nevertheless, Musser did the surveying (his wife holding the pole), the house design, and the plans. With the help of some high school students, he built the forms, poured the concrete for the foundation, and did most of the framing. He also did the siding and the roof, the plumbing and the electrical work, the redwood interior, the fireplace, the tubs and sinks, the tiles in the kitchen and bathroom and the sheetrock, its texturing and painting, the wall papering —everything! A multi-disciplinary project, indeed! He found the project most interesting, great fun, and it significantly both lowered his new families living costs and improved their lives.

With the year of house-building finished, Musser returned to his future studies. Among other necessary learning tasks, for his own use, to help him consolidate and organize much of what he was learning, he wrote a history of the known universe from the Big Bang to the present time on Earth.

Earning money, of course, always conflicted with his future efforts. While at Juilliard, going on vacation, he couldn't find anyone to feed his tropical fish. So he built a contraption out of wire and paper, powered by an old electric clock, to do the feeding. Upon his return, he found his fish alive and thriving. This got Musser quite interested in inventing. He next decided to invent the water bed. He assembled the plywood for the frame, plastic to hold the water, and the heating element to warm the water, to test the concept. But this was when he moved from New York City back to California. Though all this bed material was sent west, Musser set aside this furniture project, and Charles Hall invented the bed some ten years later.

But in California, Musser did invent, patent, manufacture, and sell a portable fireplace and barbecue that could be enjoyed on the patio in the evenings, then wheeled out of sight the following morning. This effort was mostly spring and summer work, leaving him ample time for his future project. He also invented and sold a toy called; BassAckwards, a kind of hockey game played in a shoe box with mirrors at both ends so the two players at each end could only see the pucks and sticks through the confusing mirrors.

Later, Musser found work managing a rental property. Perfect. It paid more frequently and reliably, and often took just one day a week.

This book, then, is the product of some sixty most interesting years of dedicated, persistent, multi-disciplinary effort. Indeed, perhaps the reason this book's discoveries were not made earlier by others is just the unusual breadth and depth of the effort required.

Made in the USA
Coppell, TX
16 November 2024

40394419R00160